A CLEAR AND CERTAIN FUTURE

An Integrated Life Planning Process

GLENNA S. CHEESMAN, SME

Order this book online at www.trafford.com/06-2439
or email orders@trafford.com

Most Trafford titles are also available at major online book retailers.

Note for Librarians: A cataloguing record for this book is available from Library
and Archives Canada at www.collectionscanada.ca/amicus/index-e.html

Printed in Victoria, BC, Canada.

ISBN: 978-1-4251-0681-2

*We at Trafford believe that it is the responsibility of us all, as both individuals
and corporations, to make choices that are environmentally and socially sound.
You, in turn, are supporting this responsible conduct each time you purchase a
Trafford book, or make use of our publishing services. To find out how you are
helping, please visit www.trafford.com/responsiblepublishing.html*

*Our mission is to efficiently provide the world's finest, most comprehensive
book publishing service, enabling every author to experience success.
To find out how to publish your book, your way, and have it available
worldwide, visit us online at www.trafford.com/10510*

www.trafford.com

North America & international
toll-free: 1 888 232 4444 (USA & Canada)
phone: 250 383 6864 ♦ fax: 250 383 6804
email: info@trafford.com

The United Kingdom & Europe
phone: +44 (0)1865 722 113 ♦ local rate: 0845 230 9601
facsimile: +44 (0)1865 722 868 ♦ email: info.uk@trafford.com

10 9 8 7 6 5 4

To all of you who shared your uncertainty.

Acknowledgments

This book was inspired by a conversation with a friend who had just been laid off from her job. Though she was a talented portrait painter, she had been earning her living painting walls. I encouraged her to use the enforced "free" time she was now facing to use her talent to establish a new career direction. That original conversation blossomed into this book.

During the creation of the book, I have been overwhelmed by the willingness of strangers to share their personal experiences and deepest concerns regarding their work and its impact on the rest of their life. I don't know your names, and you don't know mine, but I thank you. You are the people I met and engaged in brief conversations who shared your personal stories on a fleeting acquaintance. You are the men on vacation; the Boston jewelry designer being measured for a suit in the tailor's shop in Thailand; the long-haul truck driver on a Caribbean cruise; the retired couple who were both former Miami vice police who had successfully transitioned to new careers—and all the others.

Your stories of uncertainty and the desire for change inspired me to complete *A Clear and Certain Future: An Integrated Life Planning Process*. My frustration was that I didn't have a copy of the book ready to hand to you; you could have emerged from your vacation with a plan and peace of mind.

A heartfelt thank you to all my family and friends who endured the process of writing this book with me. Without your unconditional support, I would never have been able to stay the course.

My very special thanks to Jens who used an early draft of this book to integrate his life. Thank you for sharing your story, photos and your kind words praising the book. The May girls, Wendy and Kay, lent me their expertise and gave me their time to edit and proofread early editions—thank you.

How do you thank your 92-year-old mother for being a continual source of inspiration and subtle encouragement with those little notes at the end of her e-mails, "How is the book going, dear?" Marjorie is loved by all, and especially by me. Many thanks to my children and grandchildren who quietly supported my efforts.

Thank you to the love of my life, Jim, who was alternately ignored or subjected to my many moods; euphoria when it was going well and total despondency when it was not.

After writing these acknowledgments, I can fully empathize with the winners at award shows who are still thanking people as the music begins to play. You hope you have thanked everyone, but you are afraid you've forgotten someone. If I did, this is my special thanks to you.

Disclaimer

Many ideas are "in the air" and come to us in snippets of conversations or experiences shared. Every attempt has been made to present original wordings in the creation of this work. If it comes to your attention that this has not been accomplished, please notify the author immediately so that revisions can be made to future editions. In the same spirit, if any misuse of this material is noticed, the author would appreciate being notified.

Table of Contents

Foreword

Don't confuse your living with your life

It took over 25 years, but I have found the secret to knowing what I want to do with my life. I then looked for a way to share what I had discovered with you. I wrote this book so you can jump-start your life without paying the same price in time.

When I started, I had the underlying suspicion I didn't know exactly what I should be doing with my life. I confused what I should be doing with my life with what I should be doing for a living.

I spent years wallowing around trying to find the perfect career that matched my intelligence with my interests, something that would let me realize my full potential. After all, isn't that what we are supposed to do—find out what we want to be when we grow up. My filing cabinets bulged with advice: notes from courses, workshops and seminars, and the results of career testing and counseling. I was told, "you can do anything you want, or you should be a university professor, in public relations or on stage". I needed to narrow down my choices.

I started applying solutions without knowing what the problems were. I bought self-help, career discovery, management and leadership books. I was directed to discover my mission, passion, purpose and destiny. I could then follow my heart and work for the love of it, not for the money. I would self-actualize and have a meaningful life because it would be a waste of my life if I only visited this earth once and didn't fulfill my purpose.

The Secret: Your Unwritten Mission in Life

The secret is: Your mission has found you, so don't waste time looking for it. The activities you choose to do each day are an expression of your mission in life, not the other way around. Instead of trying to write a mission statement to live up to, start with your daily activities and see what they are telling you about your unwritten mission that is directing your daily activities.

A Clear and Certain Future is the shortcut to planning my life I wish someone had given me 25 years ago.

Introduction

It's 7:00a.m. The turquoise water is sparkling between the fronds of a palm tree. I'm sitting on the balcony in silk pajamas. The gentle morning sun is warming my body. I'm working on my research project. I have finished my work out and am feeling calm and relaxed. Later, I will e-mail family and friends to let them know I am thinking of them. My romantic partner and I will have lunch together. This afternoon, I will spend some time with the small business owners I am counseling. I feel I am doing the things that are important to me.

Wish? Or reality? Reality. My reality. How did this happen? I developed and used the two-part goal setting process to turn my wish "to live and work somewhere warm someday" into my reality.

Over the last 25 years, thousands of books have been written to help individuals solve problems and make changes in their lives. At book stores, these books are classified into how to, self–help, new age, inspiration, popular psychology, parenting and relationships. They have made their way into the sections on business and financial planning, as well as job search, career development and retirement planning. The purpose of these books is to allow you to benefit from the experience of the authors rather than spending the time to do all the research yourself.

Self-help has spawned speaking engagements and television shows that have launched the careers of several individuals who are now household names. The need for information and advice on personal and professional development continues to explode.

This book is a manual to plan your whole life. Until now, you have been offered a fragmented approach to life planning. The focus has been on one aspect of your life: your soul or purpose, your physical health or diet, your mental or emotional health, your family or romantic relationships, your finances or wealth, your friends or other people, what you do for fun, your contributions to society, and your education or your career. This book is an integrated process to plan your whole life. If you wish to explore one aspect of your life in detail, visit any book store. Many valuable sources exist for in–depth insights.

Whether you are making decisions for yourself or are assisting others as they plan some aspect of their lives, you will benefit from the information in *A Clear and Certain Future*. Using dozens of examples and exercises, this book offers comprehensive, hands-on, step-by-step advice for choosing a set of goals for a balanced life. You will find out how to:

➢ use the two-part goal setting process to search for information to solve problems and then use that information to make decisions

➢ define goal setting to clarify your understanding of the process

➢ develop a clear picture of your current situation

➢ discover who you are and how your daily Activities define who you are

➢ classify the Activities on your Someday list into the ten Keys to a Balanced Life

➢ do the things that are important to you in the 8760 hours available to you each year

➢ choose priorities, switch priorities, shift between priorities, and deal with conflicting priorities

➢ identify your potential roadblocks and detours, including other people's priorities, and measures and labels

➢ apply the resources you have and develop new resources to eliminate your roadblocks

➢ learn how to use who you are and what you do to achieve balance in your life

➢ establish small, manageable steps suited to your roadblocks and resources to make fifteen minutes of daily progress on your priority activities

➢ establish short-term and long-term plans with the power of time horizons and time lines

➢ put the act into Activities to discover your motives

➢ reveal the ten goals for a balanced life that are reflected by your daily Activities and use the vision revealed by your goals to see your future

➢ discover the unwritten Mission in Life that is guiding your everyday Activities.

About the Book

This book provides you with specific problem solving and decision-making strategies to establish an integrated set of goals that encompasses the ten Keys to a Balanced Life.

Guidance, career, and religious counselors; educators; bank, financial and retirement planners; individuals and small business owners; human resource managers and consultants; health and mental health professionals and practitioners will be given a proven method to turn a fragmented approach to life planning into an integrated set of goals for a balanced life.

Included in *A Clear and Certain Future* are four new tools specifically developed to help you with this task. They are the:

➤ two-part goal setting process

➤ Keys to a Balanced Life

➤ My Ideal Occupation tool

➤ Two Why's motivation tool

The first tool and foundation of the book is the two-part goal setting process. It simplifies goal setting by dividing it into two processes—problem solving and decision-making. The problem solving process involves answering five questions to gather information. The second part of goal setting is the eight-step decision process. This step-by-step tool uses the information you have gathered about yourself to guide you through the process of developing goals that reflect your daily activities. Once you have established your goals, you will create your unwritten mission statement.

The second tool is a set of ten keys. The ten Keys to a Balanced Life is a tool to classify all those items that you want to do someday into the ten key areas of human endeavor.

The third tool helps you find your ideal occupation. For the purposes of the My Ideal Occupation tool, an occupation is what you do to occupy your time, paid or unpaid, regardless of your age or the stage of your life.

The fourth tool is Two Why's to discover what is motivating you. Once you know what your motives are, you will know why you are doing what you are doing and why you want to do it.

Sprinkled throughout the text are Reality Checks to reinforce the key ideas that have been presented.

In this book, all the things that you do or want to do are called Activities. Other names for them are:

➤ things to do

➤ projects

➤ events

➤ items on a To Do list, or Someday list.

How to Use This Book

This is your book, about your life. Part I presents information followed by an example that illustrates the information. At the end of each section there is an exercise to record your own experiences and examples. You will collect, organize and record information to use in Part II.

To know exactly what you want to do with the rest of your life, you need a tool to sift and sort through all this information. Part II of this book is the Eight-Step Decision Process. This tool guides you through the process of developing goals that are a reflection of your daily activities.

You will need a pencil or pen, a notebook or notepad and a highlighter. A calculator is useful for adding up the times in some of the exercises. If the computer is your tool of choice, a spreadsheet program will do.

Too Soon Old, and Too Late Smart

One of my Dad's favorite expressions was "too soon old, and too late smart". What he was saying was that time passes and you don't get the information you need to make the decisions you need to make—until it is too late for you to use it to your advantage.

You now hold a tool in your hands to help you have *A Clear and Certain Future*. You will recognize the opportunities that fit with your plan for your life when they come your way. Dozens of tools, tips, techniques, exercises and examples are included to help you develop an integrated plan for your whole life.

The Two-Part Goal Setting Process

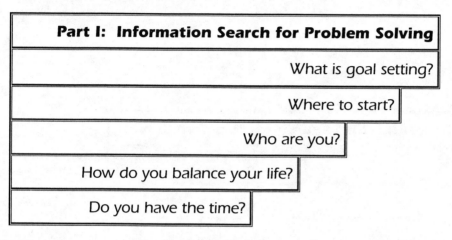

Part I: Information Search for Problem Solving

What is goal setting?

Where to start?

Who are you?

How do you balance your life?

Do you have the time?

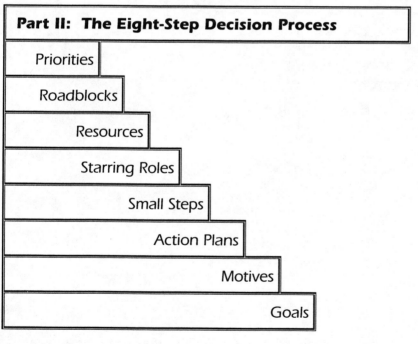

Part II: The Eight-Step Decision Process

Priorities

Roadblocks

Resources

Starring Roles

Small Steps

Action Plans

Motives

Goals

Mission in Life

PART I
INFORMATION SEARCH
FOR
PROBLEM SOLVING

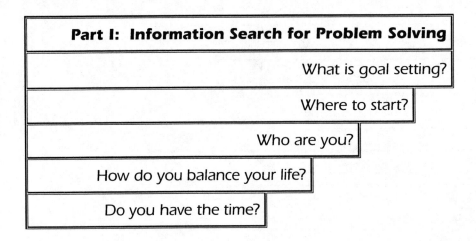

Part I: Information Search for Problem Solving
What is goal setting?
Where to start?
Who are you?
How do you balance your life?
Do you have the time?

QUESTION ONE:

What is goal setting?

The first thing you need to do is to remove the confusion surrounding goal setting. You will review your experience with goal setting in your personal and work life; learn the difference between Activities and Goals; evaluate what you don't want to do with the rest of your life, and examine the red herrings that may have thrown you off your path.

Through exercises and examples, you will learn what goal setting is and establish a definition of what goal setting means to you.

- ➤ False Goals, Fools Gold
- ➤ Who? Me?
- ➤ Ready! Set! Pause!
- ➤ Don't Miss the Training
- ➤ The "If" in Life
- ➤ Searching for Answers
- ➤ Solid Gold Nuggets of Wisdom
- ➤ Definitively Defined

✓ **REALITY CHECK**

Goal setting is a process for planned change.
It is a combination of two other processes—
problem solving and decision-making.

Example: How the word goal is used in sports

If you were at a football game and the announcer said that your team had scored a goal, there would be no doubt in your mind what had just happened. If it also happened to be the goal that won the game, you would be on your feet cheering.

Too bad it isn't as easy to know the score in life! It would be if:

➤ you knew how long you were playing

➤ everyone defined a goal in the same way

➤ everyone was playing the same game

➤ clearly defined levels of achievement existed

➤ the equipment and resources were specified

➤ the goals were worth a specific number of points

➤ a referee blew the whistle when things got out of hand

➤ you had a coach who would give you constructive criticism in the locker room at half time.

With games, complex sets of rules have been established. Everyone plays the game and counts the goals scored the same way. But life isn't like that.

False Goals, Fools Gold

Confusion surrounds goals and goal setting because the word "goal" is used to mean so many things. Activities that are part of a To Do list of things that you want or need to get done—someday—are often considered to be your goals.

Example: Your Experience

➤ Think of New Year's Eve. Many of you use this occasion to resolve to change something in your life. Quit smoking and lose weight are two of the perennial favorites. These are positive things to do, but they are too general to create any excitement about their accomplishment. These are Activities.

➤ You may have been exposed to goal setting when a workplace manager gave the directive, "you need to set some goals because we have decided we are going to change the way our performance evaluations will be conducted". Sound familiar? Without training or experience in setting goals, a normally competent employee may panic when faced with this new task.

➤ Possibly, you may have been told your goal was zero defects on a production line or the response time to the customer was going to be reduced to fifteen minutes. The problem is, of course, you had no idea if this was possible and if it was, how you would go about accomplishing it.

➤ Perhaps you think about the goals that were handed down to you by your manager. To keep you and everybody else busy, she came up with a list of

Activities. You worked to get these Activities done; but they weren't business goals, and they definitely weren't your goals.

> ➤ If you were that manager, this may have been part of your career development plan to demonstrate to your superiors that you could run a goal-oriented department. Your goal was to ensure everyone in your department had goals, but usually, they were just Activities.

Who? Me?

Depending on the level of the employee, their goals may be handed to them by their manager. Possibly, employees will be asked to formulate goals of their own in support of the manager's goals. Frequently, goal setting for the employee is a combination of both.

It is still rare within an organization to consider or integrate the employee's quality of work-life and her personal goals into this goal setting process. If their employees have never been asked to participate in this process before, good leaders recognize the need to carefully develop a plan to introduce this process to them. Goal setting is a skill that can be taught, and learned.

Ready! Set! Pause!

Your ability to assume a new task depends on your training. It doesn't matter whether you need to set goals, learn a new computer program or perform brain surgery; you have to have knowledge, technical skills and confidence in your ability to successfully complete the task. Even though you may be interested in it and willing to undertake it, until you have the ability to do it, you are going to be on a steep learning curve before you reach the point where you are comfortable with this new task.

Don't Miss the Training

It is up to the manager to provide their employees with the confidence they need to be involved in the goal setting process. Training to communicate the required knowledge and skills must be completed before the employees are asked to do it.

✓ REALITY CHECK

Employees need to have the information in this book
before
they become involved in the goal setting process.

The "If" in Life

If you ask yourself "what do I want to do with the rest of my life?" you may start your list with what you don't want to do. It could be what you are doing now, or what your parents or someone else did. Somehow you know these are things you don't want for the rest of your life. So, how do you discover what you do want?

Example: What you don't want to do with the rest of your life

I don't want to spend it doing what I am doing now.

Turn it into a positive.

I want to spend my life _____.

You fill in the blank.

If you can't fill in the blank now—don't worry—you will be able to when you have finished this book.

Searching for Answers

When you are searching for what you should be doing with your life, red herrings can waste your time. A red herring is something that causes you to leave your chosen path, temporarily, or permanently. Red herrings are tempting. A quick little morning read of your horoscope, or a one-hour session with a palm reader on Saturday afternoon, creates the illusion that there are greater forces at work. Your life is under control and is unfolding according to a master plan.

Technology has supplied a new red herring. Many of the e-mails you receive each week ask you to get to know yourself or your friends. If you have the time, these are fun to do, and they can provide a temporary distraction from whatever it was you were focusing on before you opened the e-mail. In Question Four, you can add the Activity "open and do fun e-mails without guilt" as one of your "Fun" Activities. Just don't count on them to supply you with a new life-changing revelation.

Having a set of goals keeps you focused on what you do want to do with your life. When you are searching for answers, you may turn to external sources to see the future, such as:

➤ A daily or weekly horoscope, an astrologer

➤ A Chinese horoscope, the I Ching

➤ A palm reader, a tea leaf reader

➤ Tarot Cards

➢ Numerology

➢ A Ouiji board, a crystal ball

➢ Dream interpretation.

What all of these sources have in common is that they are based on the premise that there is some secret truth that exists but it is hidden from you. By getting in touch with universal forces, the truth will be revealed. It is in the stars or on the cards.

They also suggest that you are incapable of making decisions for yourself. These Activities cost you time, and usually money; however, if you keep them in perspective, they can also be one of the things you do for "Fun".

To evaluate the value, to you, of these external sources, ask yourself these questions:

➢ Would I seriously change my life based on a prediction?

➢ Do these sources expand or limit my options?

➢ Do I really want to relinquish control of my life?

➢ Have I become a self-fulfilling prophecy?

➢ Have I eliminated people from my life based on their supposed incompatibility with me?

➢ Have these external sources provided answers to my questions about what I want to do with my life?

Without a good alternative, you may have embraced these external sources as a valid source of information for what you should do with your life. Up until now, you lacked a starting point and a structure for your plan. You had too much information or you lacked useful information about yourself. You needed a logical process to filter all the information and organize it into a usable format. The two-part goal setting process provides you with an easy step-by-step framework.

Getting to know yourself at this level is a lot of work and requires a commitment of a minimum of 24 hours to read this book and do the exercises. However, this is your future—aren't you worth it?

A Clear and Certain Future places the control of your life firmly in your hands. With enough useful information about yourself and a decision-making system to use that information, you can show yourself your own future.

Solid Gold Nuggets of Wisdom

➢ Goal setting is the result of conscious and thoughtful decisions. Your goals focus your time on achieving specific results that are a reflection of what you want to do with your life. You choose your own set of goals from all the possible activities that you as a human could engage in. What you choose to do is unique to you and your circumstances.

➤ Choosing goals involves making choices and eliminating other options. In other words, choosing goals involves making decisions. You may feel that choosing goals is in some way limiting. You may be afraid to choose a set of goals because you don't want to be limited in what you can and can't do. The result is that you try to keep your options open indefinitely.

The irony is, that by choosing goals, your options are actually broadened. Once you have committed to a goal, you will achieve it. You can then work on the next goal on your list. You will get more of the important things done.

✓ REALITY CHECK

Goals need to be written and reviewed often.

➤ Written goals get accomplished. Review your progress monthly.

➤ Written goals are not written in concrete like your name on your sidewalk. They provide a focus and direction for your daily Activities. A set of written goals clarifies what is important to you.

If you write them, start them, and then find out they aren't working for you, you can re-evaluate them. In Part II, Step One, you will learn how to identify conflicting priorities and Step Eight includes what to do if you don't accomplish your goals.

➤ Goals have different time horizons attached to them—some are short-term and some are long-term. Goals can require giving up something now, to gain something later.

➤ Personal goal setting is a life-long process. As you achieve one set of goals, you choose new goals, accomplish them and choose new goals.

You don't have to tell anyone what your goals are unless you need their cooperation. People can be a roadblock or a resource. Try to keep the number of goals that require other people's involvement to a minimum.

✓ REALITY CHECK

Goal setting is something you can learn,
and as with most things,
you get better with practice.

Goal Setting Definitively Defined

To eliminate all the confusion, start by defining what goal setting means to you. This is your own definition; using words you choose to clarify this Activity of "Goal Setting".

Below are two lists of words that can be substituted for "goal" and for "set". You may have heard these other words used instead of goal setting.

How is the word "goal" defined?

LIST ONE	OTHER WORDS THAT MEAN THE SAME THING
Goal	objective, aim, end, ambition, purpose, target, object, aspiration
Objective	object, point, purpose, aim, idea, goal, intention, intent.

You can use a dictionary or thesaurus to define the words "goal" and "set" to your own satisfaction. These are suggestions to get you started.

What does it mean to 'set' a goal?

LIST TWO	OTHER WORDS THAT MEAN THE SAME THING
Set	establish, put in writing, make firm
Establish	fix, agree, appoint, decide, settle on, arrange
Decide	make a decision, come to a decision, make up your mind, choose, settle on, fix on, resolve.

Example: Define the Activity of Goal Setting

I am going to choose my set of goals.

There are many options that could be included in the choice set. You must decide what to include from all of the options that are available to you as a human being. Some of your alternatives must be postponed for now, if not forever. In Part II of this book, you will decide which options you will include in your choice set.

Exercise: Your Definition of Goal Setting

Copy the following sentence onto a blank sheet of paper, or into a blank document on your computer. Choose one word from LIST TWO and enter it in the first blank. Choose one word from LIST ONE and write it in the second blank.

I am going to _____ (enter your List Two Word) my ____
_____ (enter your List One Word)

You have now defined what goal setting means to you. Post it somewhere where you will see it each day. This is your commitment to add the Activity of Goal Setting to your life.

QUESTION TWO:

Where to start?

The challenge in getting something done is to know where to start. Knowing where to start depends on where you are starting from today. Everyone's situation will be different. Decisions you have made created the situation that is now the starting point for the rest of your life. This section looks at your current situation and the decision-making style that brought you to where you are today.

➢ Your Current Situation

➢ Decisions! Decisions! Decisions!

➢ Suspending Judgment

Your Current Situation

Where you are today is a point in time somewhere between your birth and your death. You know when you arrived, but you don't know when you will leave. If that seems to be a rather blunt statement to you, it is meant to be. Life can change in a heartbeat. Recognize the urgency of getting on with what you want to do with your life. Develop the awareness that you are making decisions all the time.

Example:

Things (Activities) as simple as deciding to have a salad instead of pasta, an apple instead of a pastry, or to walk to the store instead of driving will all have a long-term impact on your life. Unless you have consciously decided to make healthful decisions, you are making random decisions and will end up with entirely different results.

Not all decisions are this simple.

Decisions! Decisions! Decisions!

Many of the decisions about what you have done (Activities), who you did it with (your Roles), and when you did it (the Time it took) may have been:

➢ random, it seemed like the right thing to do at the time

➢ just going with the flow

➤ not making waves

➤ to meet other people's expectations or priorities

➤ to satisfy feelings of:

- obligation

- duty

- guilt

- desperation.

At some points in your life, you focused your time and energy on a single event. Some of these events may have been:

➤ Graduating, changing jobs or careers

➤ Buying, selling or building a new residence

➤ Moving to a new location for education or work

➤ Getting married or the arrival of a baby

➤ Planning a vacation or your retirement.

These events (Activities) took time and became all-consuming as you focused on the details needed for their completion. All your other Activities were viewed in the context of how they related to or impacted your current focus.

✓ REALITY CHECK

These were Activities you chose to do.
Each had an underlying goal.

At other times, a sudden crisis may have refocused your attention, and therefore, your time, if:

➤ you were laid off from your job

➤ your health failed

➤ a family member had a medical crisis

➤ a relationship ended

➤ a loved one passed away

➤ a natural disaster occurred.

Your life has been full of planned, and unplanned, events (Activities). You may have said, "that's just the way life is—everyone's life is a series of events that throws him off-balance and that he has to react to". When a sudden crisis occurred, yes this was true; but in the rest of your life you made the decisions.

Suspending Judgment

Do not attach a judgment to your current situation. It is where you are today—period. It is the starting point for the rest of your life.

You cannot change the past. What is done is done. Your awareness of what you have control over versus what has control over you will help you to realize the importance of making thoughtful and conscious, rather than random decisions. The sections on Roadblocks and Resources in Part II will clarify the issue of control.

The following example could be two people, two decisions at one point in time. Or it could be one person, one point in time, two decisions.

Example: Where you are today

Situation One:

> **Where you are today:**
> Visiting my parents
> **Planned / Consciously Made Decision:**
> Yes
> **Crisis or some other reason:**
> Out of guilt, because I live out of town and I feel as if I have been selfish by making my interests more important than devoting time to my parents.

Situation Two:

> **Where you are today:**
> Traveling and writing
> **Planned / Consciously Made Decision:**
> Yes
> **Crisis or some other reason:**
> I retired to pursue my hobby of writing and am doing exactly what I want to do with the rest of my life.

Now it's your turn to list as many situations as you need to:

➢ clarify your current situation

➢ consider the decisions you have made and why you made them

➢ ask yourself if you are doing what you want to do.

This exercise identifies some of the decisions you have made that resulted in you being where you are today. It serves as a starting point for the changes you want to make in your life. There are some areas of your life that you are happy with, but there are other areas where you want to make changes. If you were contented with your life as you are living it today, you would not want to make any changes.

Exercise: Where You Are Today

Make a list or a brief statement about where you feel you are today.

You:

➤ Where you are today:

➤ Planned / Consciously Made Decision: Yes or No

➤ Crisis or some other reason: Yes or No

Your situation is the result of decisions you have made to choose one Activity instead of another. Each Activity required you to accept a Role that went with it. In the next section, you will look at the roles you play in your life.

QUESTION THREE:

Who are you? Role Call

All of the Activities you do in your life on a day-to-day basis are done in one of your roles. You switch roles constantly. If you feel you are stretched too thin, you have taken on too many roles at the same time. Each Activity has a role attached to it. Activities use time. Your time is all you have. Identify the roles you have taken on to answer the question "Who Am I?" This section covers the many roles that you could have.

- ➤ What is a Role?
- ➤ Interactive Roles and Independent Roles
- ➤ Interactive Roles
  - Domino Roles
  - Primary Roles
  - Secondary Roles
  - Community Roles
- ➤ Roles-within-Roles
- ➤ Role Models
- ➤ Independent Roles
  - On Being an Individual
  - Independent Role – Individual Activities
    - ○ Independent Roles-within-Roles
      - Independent Roles – Individual Activities – Consumer
        - ❏ Consumer – Roles-within-Roles.

What is a Role?

When you talk to your friends about the movie you just saw, they ask, "Who was in that?" Your favorite actor or actress plays one role in today's movie, and a different role in the one you watch tomorrow. Actors can change roles frequently and can thoughtfully and consciously choose which roles to play.

You, however, do not choose many of the roles you have and yet these same roles stay with you for your entire life. You have roles that are connected to the Activities you choose. Later, you will learn how you have five or more roles just by being born.

Interactive Roles and Independent Roles

Roles are convenient labels that are used to explain who you are interacting with when you choose to do an Activity. You relate to the members of your family in Family Roles. You have other relationships that require other roles.

Activities, and their associated roles, are either Interactive—in relationships with others, or Independent—on your own. In your Interactive Roles, you devote yourself to maintaining the relationships you have established and spend your time doing Activities in those roles. Sometimes, you have the role but don't maintain the relationship.

Your Independent Role is the Role of Individual. There are many things that can or must be done on your own. This is you, as an Individual, choosing to do Activities for and by yourself. For example, if you separated the Activities on your To Do list, how many are for, or with, other people? How many are just for you?

There are some people in your life that you would label as "selfish or self-centered". Their Interactive Roles are neglected as they spend their time thinking only of themselves. The ten Keys to a Balanced Life will help you to choose between Interactive and Independent Activities and Roles.

Interactive Roles

In the Role of Son or Daughter, you are committed to your parents and make a point of keeping in touch with them. You spend time doing Activities with them. On the other hand, you may have cousins you haven't seen or talked to for over forty years. The strength of your family ties are based on the emotional bonds the individuals have formed with one another, usually through years of regular contact. Other times, you may have formed instant friendships and these people become "like family" to you.

The Interactive Roles you have can be viewed as Primary Roles, Secondary Roles, and Community Roles. Your Primary and Secondary Roles have Domino Roles. Your roles can also be viewed from the perspective of Roles of No Choice and Roles of Choice.

Interactive Domino Roles

Domino Roles are inherited, not chosen, Family Roles. They are roles that result from your Primary and Secondary Roles.

Example: Domino Roles: No Choice

When you were born, you inherited parents and grandparents. You possibly inherited a sister or brother. If your parents had a sister or brother, you inherited an aunt or uncle and the role of niece or nephew. If your aunt or uncle had a child, you had no choice—you inherited the role of cousin.

Interactive Primary Roles

Primary Roles arrived with you when you were born. You had no choice whether you accepted these roles or not. They came from being a member of a group you must interact with, the Family. When you arrived, you were your parent's daughter or son.

Family Primary Roles – Roles of No Choice and their Domino Roles of No Choice

No Choice   Your Parents decide to have you
1. Daughter or Son
   Activities and Time to maintain the relationships with your

   ➢ Mother (1)

   ➢ Father (2)

No Choice   Your Parents each have a living mother and father
Domino Family Role
2. Grand-daughter or Grandson
   Activities and Time to maintain the relationships with your

   ➢ Grandmothers
   Mother's Mother (3)
   Father's Mother (4)

   ➢ Grandfathers
   Mother's Father (5)
   Father's Father (6)
   Living Great-grandparents create additional Roles and Relationships.

No Choice   *Your Parents have or decide to have an additional child or children*
Domino Family Role
3. Sister or Brother
     Activities and Time to maintain the relationships with your

  ➢ Sister(s) (7)

  ➢ Brother(s) (8)

No Choice   *Your Parents have sisters and brothers*
Domino Family Role
4. Niece or Nephew
     Activities and Time to maintain the relationships with your

  ➢ Aunt(s) and Uncle(s) (9)

No Choice   *Your Parents' Sisters or Brothers have or decide to have a child or children*
Domino Family Role
5. Cousin
     Activities and Time to maintain the relationships with your

  ➢ Cousin(s) (10)

No Choice   *Your Sisters or Brothers are married or decide to get married*
Domino Family Role
6. Sister-in-law / Brother-in-law
     Activities and Time to maintain the relationships with your

  ➢ Sister(s) or Brother(s)-in-law (11)

No Choice   *Your Sisters or Brothers have, or decide to have a child or children*
Domino Family Role
7. Aunt or Uncle
     Activities and Time to maintain the relationships with your

  ➢ Niece(s) and nephew(s) (12)

No Choice   *Your Niece(s) or Nephew(s) decide to get married*
Domino Family Role
8. Aunt or Uncle
     Activities and Time to maintain the relationships with your

  ➢ Niece(s) and nephew(s) spouse (13)

No Choice   Your Niece(s) or Nephew(s) decide to have a child or children
Domino Family Role
9. Grand Aunt or Grand Uncle
    Activities and Time to maintain the relationships with your

> ➤ Niece(s) and nephew(s) child or children (14)

Interactive Secondary Roles

Secondary Roles are Family Roles that arise from choices you make, or made, during the course of your life. You did have a choice as to whether you would get involved romantically with someone. When you make the choice to step into Secondary Roles, you assume a whole new set of Domino Roles as well.

Family Secondary Roles – Roles of Choice and their Domino Roles of No Choice

Choice Decision to get involved in a romantic relationship
Secondary Family Role
10. Romantic Partner
    Activities and Time to maintain the relationship with your

> ➤ Romantic Partner (15)

Choice Decision to formalize the romantic relationship
Leads to No Choice
Domino Family Role
11. Daughter / Son-in-law
    Activities and Time to maintain the relationships with your

> ➤ Partner's Mother-
>   Your Mother-in-law(16)

> ➤ Partner's Father-
>   Your Father-in-law(17)

No Choice   When you formalize your romantic relationship, if your partner has sister(s) or brother(s)
Domino Family Role
12. Sister / Brother-in-law
    Activities and Time to maintain the relationships with

> ➤ Your Partner's Sister(s) or Brother(s)(18)

> ➤ Their mate(s) (if they have one)(19)

➢ Relation-in-marriage to
Your partner's Aunts, (20) Uncles, (21) Cousins, (22) Grandparents, (23)

You inherit a whole new set of roles when you decide to have children.

Choice Decision to have a child/children
Secondary Family Role
13. Mother / Father
    Activities and Time to maintain the relationships with your

➢ Child/Children (24)

Then, when your children decide to change their roles, you inherit another set of roles.

No Choice   *Your child/children decide to formalize a romantic relationship*
Domino Family Role
14. Mother-in-law / Father-in-law
    Activities and Time to maintain the relationships with your

➢ Child/children's mate(s) (25)
  (Daughter-in-law, Son-in-law)

No Choice   *Decision by your child/children to have a child/children*
Domino Family Role
15. Grandmother / Grandfather
    Activities and Time to maintain the relationships with your

➢ Grandchild/Grandchildren (26)

No Choice   *Your Sister(s)/Brother(s)-in-law have a child /children or decide to have a child/ children*
Domino Family Role
16. Aunt / Uncle
    Activities and Time to maintain the relationships with your

➢ Sister(s)/Brother(s)-in-law's children, your niece(s)/nephew(s) (27)

Interactive Community Roles

Community Roles are usually Roles of Choice. Community Roles are Interactive Roles outside of the Family and in society at large. You choose your Community Roles, except when you are young and your parents make your decisions for you.

Community Roles—Roles of Choice

Choice Decision to make friends

17. Friend

Activities and Time to maintain the relationships with your

➤ Friend(s) (28)

Choice Decision to get an education

18. Student / Learner

Activities and Time to maintain the relationships with your

➤ Instructor(s) (29)

➤ Classmates (possible friendships) (30)

Choice Decision to get a job

19. Worker

Activities and Time to maintain the relationships with your

➤ Employer (31)

➤ Co-workers (possible friendships) (32)

Choice Decision to join with other people

20. Group, Organization, Club Member or Volunteer

Activities and Time to maintain the relationships with your

➤ Members (teammates) (33)

➤ Recipients of volunteer activities (34)

➤ Organized religion (35)

You can have some, or all, of these roles. Your interactive relationships can create twenty or more roles. You step into these twenty roles when you choose to do Activities and spend time to maintain the thirty-five relationships outlined above. Each Role can involve more than one relationship. Not all of the relationships are counted here.

Example: Your Roles and Relationships

In the role of friend, you do Activities and spend time to maintain each friendship. You can choose to do different Activities with each friend, but if you have five good friends you make an effort to spend time with them. One role, five relationships, many Activities.

In these days of blended families, Roles and Relationships multiply.

Roles-within-Roles

Breaking down your roles into Roles-within-Roles helps you to further identify how you see yourself.

Romantic Partner   wife / husband, partner, playmate, lover, travel companion, social hostess
Mother / Father   teacher, chauffeur, doctor, counselor
Worker   by what your job title (label) is
          accountant, chef, writer or Certified Public Accountant, Executive Chef or mystery writer
Group or Club Member, Volunteer – by organization
          Brownies / Guides / Scouts, little league coach, school volunteer, service club member, camp counselor
Group or Club Member, by what you do
          choir member, member of a congregation, book or fitness club member, association member
Group or Club Member, by what you play
          player on a hockey or baseball team, golf club member

These roles all represent Activities that are using your time and keeping you busy.

Role Models

There are an unlimited number of roles you can choose for yourself, in addition to those you inherit. There might be an actor who has characteristics you admire or the character an actor plays could be your Role Model. You could have met or know about other people who you use as your Role Models.

Role Models have characteristics you admire or they have achieved things you want to achieve for yourself. When you are identifying your roles, include any of your roles that are modeled after someone else.

No matter how much you admire them; Role Models are "Other People". You measure yourself against, and compare yourself to, them and their accomplishments. In Part II, Other People as a Roadblock or Resource are discussed in detail.

Make a note of any Role Model(s) you have.

My Role Model (s) is / are _____.

I admire _____(this)_____ about him or her.

Your Independent Role

The only Independent Role you have is as an Individual. When you are alone, or are engaging in your own interests, you are acting independently. Some of you choose to sail solo around the world; others will choose to work in their garden.

As an Individual you engage in Activities within society but not with other people. These are called personal Activities. These Activities result in Roles-within-Roles as an Individual. Some of these roles are labeled and some are not. You could call yourself an Exerciser, a Jogger or a TV Watcher, but not a Sleeper, an Eater or a Tooth brusher.

Independent Role: Individual Activities

➤ Maintain Your Physical Self   Sleep, eat, groom, exercise, vacation

➤ Maintain Your Spirit   Spiritual rejuvenation

➤ Maintain Your Finances   Financial planning

➤ Maintain Your Possessions   House, car, animal, garden

➤ Take a Mental Holiday   Watch TV, read fiction or the newspaper

➤ Express Yourself   Use your skills and talents, explore your interests, immerse yourself in spiritual celebration, have an adventure vacation

Individual: Roles-Within-Roles

Your Individual Roles-within-Roles are really Activities, or things that you do. Because these Activities represent a use of your time, and can be labeled, they are roles that you have as an individual. These are things you can, or must do on your own.

Example: Activities that are labeled as roles

Individual – by skills, talents, interests
          reader, writer, artist, athlete—golfer, hiker, biker, gardener, decorator, woodworker, genealogy researcher

Individual – by things you do
          cook, cleaner, shopper, dishwasher, worshipper, appreciator of nature

Individual – consumer

The Role of Consumer has many Roles-within-Roles.

Independent Role Individual: Consumer

In your Role of Consumer, you interact with society, as an Individual. In some interactions, you have a friendly relationship with the service provider; however, you would not usually consider him as a friend.

Example: **Service providers you deal with that are not friends would be:**

➢ your hairdresser, mechanic, retail clerks

➢ the bartender or the desk clerk at the hotel where you stay on business or vacation.

As a Consumer, you use your time and your money to purchase goods and services to maintain, secure and beautify yourself, your family, your vehicles, where you live, your garden, your pet and to entertain yourself, as well as to travel to a destination.

Example: **Consumer – Roles-within-Roles**

➢ Car owner, car driver, car washer

➢ Renter, homeowner, bill payer, tax payer

➢ Gardener, decorator, do-it-yourselfer, pet owner

➢ Movie or concert attendee, diner, drinker, sports fan

➢ Traveler, tourist, commuter if not under Worker.

Much of the time, it seems there is too much to do, and not enough time to do it. You may have said, "I just don't have time for myself" or "I don't have time to think". This is the time to identify your Roles, Interactive and Independent, the Activities you do, and the time these Activities use.

It could be that you are taking time for yourself, but you have allowed your personal (Independent/Individual) Activities to become items on your To Do list, rather than appreciating the time you are devoting to yourself.

Example: To Do for You

➢ Go to the gym—for your physical well-being

➢ Get my hair cut—for your physical appearance

➢ Weed the garden—to nurture your soul if it was your idea to have a garden

➢ Walk the dog—for fun if it is your dog and not something you are doing for someone else.

Exercise: Your Interactive and Independent Roles

Interactive Roles

➢ Use the method you have chosen – notebook, computer or grids - and write down your Interactive Roles – Family: Primary, Secondary, Domino and your Community Roles: Student, Volunteer, Friend, Organization / Group Member.

➢ Include Roles-within-Roles. In Appendix C, sample grids are available for you to copy.

➢ Take all the time you need.

➢ Include every Role as it occurs to you.

Independent Roles

Record your Roles-within-Roles and the Consumer Roles you have as an Individual.

In Question Five, you will write down the Activities you do in your roles. If you think of an Activity you do that doesn't fit with one of the roles you have listed, record the Activity and match it with a role later.

You may wish to list all of your roles on a sheet of paper, and then transfer them onto a grid. You may prefer to use a notebook and list each Role on a separate page or use a spreadsheet program on the computer. Do what works for you. Sample grids are available in Appendix C.

If additional roles come to mind as you continue to read, go back and add them to your list. Each Activity you do is done in one of your roles. Activities consume time. Time is all you have. In the next section, you will learn about the ten Keys to a Balanced Life.

QUESTION FOUR:

How do you balance your life?

Unlock the Secret to a Balanced Life

All of your Activities and their associated roles take place in one of the ten Keys to a Balanced Life. Until you are aware of these ten keys, your Activities are random items on a To Do list. When you have a set of goals, the Activities on your To Do list become the Small Steps that move you toward the accomplishment of your goals.

The focus in this section is on the Activities on your Someday lists, not the items on your To Do lists. To Do lists will be renamed and will become Small Steps in Part II.

Goal Setting—the Activity—may be on your Someday list as something you want to do. Goal setting must be made a priority and be permanently removed from your Someday list. It must become one of your #1 Priority Activities. It is an ongoing process. You will accomplish your goals and need to set new goals. It is the way to have a balanced life. In this section, you will learn

> ➤ what the ten Keys to a Balanced Life are

> ➤ how to turn someday into one day

> ➤ the difference between To Do lists and Someday lists

> ➤ what you want to be when you grow up

> ➤ what you want to do with the limited time you will be allowed to spend here on planet earth

> ➤ how to find the occupation that may be your vocation as well.

Turning Someday into One Day

You are never too old to try something new. My grandmother and mother are perfect examples of this. Grandma started oil painting at 84. She had her first one-man show at 86. My mother's passion is genealogical research. At 86, she bought her first computer and took lessons so it would be easier to find new information on the family.

—G. S. Cheesman

Is it a To Do List or a Someday List?

The difference between a To Do list and a Someday list is that most of the items on a To Do list are maintenance items. These Activities are the small steps that move you toward the accomplishment of a greater goal. You will learn what your goals are in Part II.

A Someday list is a list of your wishes, hopes, dreams and plans that were postponed as you became too busy living to have a life.

To Do Lists

A To Do list has "things to do" with an immediate, or short-term, planning horizon. These are Activities you want to do today or this week. Once you have learned what your goals are, you will see how the daily Activities that keep you busy are a reflection of what is important to you.

Example: To Do List

To Do Today

- ➤ Get my hair cut
- ➤ Put gas in the car
- ➤ Buy a birthday gift
- ➤ Meet Joan for lunch
- ➤ Get groceries

Once you classify the Activities on your To Do list under the ten keys, it might look like this:

To Do Today

- ➤ Get my hair cut   Key: Physical Health

  Role: Independent: Individual/Consumer
- ➤ Put gas in the car   Key: Mental Health

  Role: Independent: Individual/Consumer/Car owner
- ➤ Buy a birthday present Key: Family

  Role: Interactive: Primary/Domino/Brother
- ➤ Meet Joan for lunch   Key: Socializing

  Role: Interactive: Community/Friend

➤ Get groceries   Key: Physical Health

                            Role: Independent: Individual/Consumer/Shopper

Someday Lists

You all have Someday lists of things you want to do; things that didn't get done last year and got moved forward onto lists of things you want to do someday. As the years passed, the list grew.

These lists float around in your brain or they are a written list you have filed away somewhere. You don't believe you will ever get a chance to do some of these activities. Time kept passing and you moved a few of the things you wanted to do when you were much younger to a "can't do" list. Examine this "can't do" list carefully and ensure that it is not a mental roadblock that is holding you back. Seniors do skydive!

In the next exercise, you will

1) get your Someday lists out from your brain or wherever else they are now.

2) classify the Activities on these lists into the ten areas of human activity that encompass a balanced life.

Classifying your Someday lists can be a revealing exercise. You end up with a list of Activities categorized under the ten keys. Where it gets surprising and sometimes scary is when you realize how many of the Activities you want to do fall under one or two of the keys.

This exercise clarifies one or more things:

1) you are neglecting parts of your life

2) your life is out of balance and where it is out of balance

3) the Activities on your Someday list that remain undone

4) you are already living a balanced life

5) you are counting on having a someday.

Whether you are planning your career, your retirement or your life, plan to include Activities in each of the keys to have balance in your life. The examples that follow the descriptions of each key offer suggestions for the type of Activities that might be included on a Someday list.

At some point you may have said, "I don't know what I want to be when I grow up" or "what am I going to do with the rest of my life?" This is a sign of two things:

1) you still have things you want to do someday

2) you have a feeling you are not doing what you "are supposed to be doing" with your life.

Living with an evolving set of goals contributes to your certainty that you are doing exactly what you want to do with your life.

We'll start by looking at each of the ten keys in detail.

The Ten Keys to a Balanced Life

1   Physical Health

2   Mental Health

3   Money

4   Fun

5   Good for My Soul

6   Family

7   Occupation

8   Socializing

9   Giving Back to Society

10 Learning

The Ten Keys to a Balanced Life

Physical Health

As an individual with good physical health, you maintain yourself in good physical condition. You can do this through eating right, exercising, having regular check-ups and avoiding situations and substances that are harmful to your health.

The daily personal maintenance Activities you engage in are time-consuming, but they help fulfill your requirement for good Physical Health and contribute to your Mental Health. Personal Maintenance Activities would include showering, grooming, shoe polishing and all the little things you do to improve your personal appearance.

Your Physical Health is the most important contributor to how much time you have, and what you can do with that time. If you are fit and healthy, more of the things you want to do someday will be possible. There is more joy in living a long time if you can get out of bed each morning to do something with your day.

Mental Health

> If the car was always dirty and out of gas, the cat's litter box hadn't been changed for two weeks, the cupboards were empty, the sink was full of moldy dishes, the laundry basket was full of dirty clothes, none of your shirts had buttons and your bank account was overdrawn, it would be a sure sign you need some balance in your life.
> —G. S. Cheesman

When these aspects of your life are out of control, it is time to examine where you are spending your time. Are you producing the positive results you desire in your life?

You acquire things and have financial affairs to preserve in a good state of order and repair. Looking after the possessions you have acquired preserves your financial investment and is also a reflection of your state of mental health. How you and your possessions look and function and the state of your financial affairs are a direct result of the maintenance activities you engage in.

These maintenance activities are the result of thoughts you have and emotions you feel. They result in your behavior, or the things you do.

Your Mental Health is the major contributor to your emotional health. The thoughts you think control the emotions you have. For every thought, you choose how you will react emotionally. Your reaction is your behavior. When you control your thoughts, you control your emotions and your behavior.

Love is one of the emotional reactions to a set of stimuli. You have thoughts, you feel emotions, and you say and do loving things toward the object of your affection.

If you change your thoughts and become critical of the object of your affection, your emotions change and your behavior changes.

You can love many different animate and inanimate objects.

1) your children

2) your spousal equivalent

3) other family members

4) your pet

5) your vehicle

6) your job

7) your house

8) your sport

9) a vacation destination

10) money

✓ REALITY CHECK

Do not love things that cannot love you back.

Love is used interchangeably with "really like" instead of using more descriptive verbs.

Example:
 I love my car.
 I really like my car because my car:

 ➢ represents a financial commitment

 ➢ is beautifully designed

 ➢ is my favorite color

 ➢ is a source of enjoyment because I can express my creativity customizing it

 ➢ contributes to my esteem needs when others admire it.

When you set goals, it is a Mental Health Activity. You remove uncertainty at the same time as you add focus and direction to your life.

Money

As a consumer, you need money. The trade-off is the more things you need, the more money you need, and the less time you have for other things in your life because you have to work more hours, days and years.

Some of you are "waiting to win the lottery". If you had all the money you needed, what would it allow you to do? This is you having an income and a level of expenses sufficient for your needs. You define what your needs are and how much is enough.

Consider:

1) how much money is enough money.

2) what you need versus what you want. Are your needs sacrificed at the expense of your wants?

3) why you want what you want.

Money is a unit of exchange. You provide something of value—your knowledge, skills, talents and your time—in exchange for money. Some of you may work at two or three jobs to make enough money to satisfy your wants and needs.

✓ REALITY CHECK

Read the section "How Are You Doing?" in Part Two, Step Two
to evaluate how you are measuring yourself.
Ask yourself why you are using that particular measure.

If your Someday list includes "pay off all my bills", don't forget it was choices and decisions you made that created those bills in the first place. Bills have to be kept in perspective for what they really are.

Bills represent:

➢ things you have purchased to make yourself or someone else happy such as gifts for birthdays or other occasions, food, drink, items for your home or children, cars, furniture

➢ payments for privileges that are available and you have allowed yourself to have, such as:

● owning an automobile which brings with it costs in the form of license, insurance, gas and maintenance

- owning a home with a mortgage, insurance, taxes and property improvements
- conveniences such as having your own phone, computer, internet connection, and cable TV
- comfort in the way of utility bills to heat or cool your environment, to light your darkness and to operate all your appliances.

➤ contributions to enjoy the benefits of the society you have chosen to be a part of in the form of income tax, other taxes and medical premiums.

Managing your cash flow—cash in/cash out—is your responsibility and is under your control. If you need some help, there are many resources available in your community; therefore, they are not included here.

✓ REALITY CHECK

The more ambitious your aspirations are, and the more wide-ranging your wants, the more money you are going to need. The more you spend, the more you have to work to earn. More things won't necessarily make you happier.

Fun

What do you, as an Individual, do for fun? Fun is some enjoyable activity that is just for fun. It is an activity you do when nothing, or no one, else is placing demands on your time. You can have fun by yourself. When you are in one of your Interactive Roles, Fun becomes Socializing.

You are more likely to take time for fun if you make it a priority. Usually fun has the elements of exploration and play. You can have fun in endless ways. Some of the things you might include in your list follow.

Fun often has the word "play" in it.

➤ Play an instrument

➤ Play a sport

➤ Play a game.

Sometimes Fun has the word "learn" in it and often Fun is a creative outlet.

➤ Learn about antiques

➤ Learn about my family tree

➤ Learn how to decorate.

Sometimes Fun is active.

➤ Dance

➤ Walk, hike, bike

➤ Shop.

Sometimes Fun is passive.

➤ Have coffee and people watch

➤ Go to a movie or a sporting event

➤ Go to the theatre or an art gallery.

Sometimes Fun is mental.

➤ Do crossword puzzles, other word games or play Solitaire

➤ Play computer games or read e-mails

➤ Read a book not related to work.

Some of you earn your living doing some of these things. Can you change your attitude toward something you are doing so it becomes fun and enjoyable even if you have called it work up until now? Is there something you do for fun you could turn into a way to occupy your hours and make money too?

Good for My Soul

What makes you say, "That was good for my soul" or "that lifted my spirits"? Spiritual celebration by yourself or with a group is a vital element in a balanced life. Commit time to connect with and nurture your inner self or soul. Your emotional health and well-being grow out of nurturing your soul. In the section on mental health, emotional strength was contributed to carefully choosing the thoughts you have and then how you react to those thoughts. Nurture your soul to change your reactions.

Family

Your first roles are in your Family group, and they expand over time. Even as you become independent of the family and evolve into an Individual, your primary Role as a child remains one of the strongest bonds. For many, the next strongest is the role of parent.

Your Family can be your greatest source of security, belonging, and joy if you make preserving your family relationships a priority. Parents need to be needed and think of you as one of the kids—well into your 30's, 40's, and 50's. Brothers and sisters have different perspectives on the same memories. Children reject your authority but remind you of what you value, and grandchildren confirm how good it feels to be the source of wisdom.

Occupation

What are you going to be when you grow up?

When you were a child, there was always some grown-up who asked, "What are you going to be when you grow up?" Even as a child, you interpreted this question as "What work are you going to do?" You dutifully answered based on your limited experience in the world, "Teacher, Doctor, Nurse, Policeman, Garbage Truck Driver, Hockey Player" or perhaps your answer was whatever your father or mother did for a living.

Because so many "grown-ups" asked "What are you going to be when you grow up?" this question was imprinted on your brain as "the question to answer". You never considered asking those grown-ups "How will I know when I am grown-up?" or "What does it mean to be grown-up?"

So as the years passed you relentlessly attempted to answer the question "What am I going to be when I grow up?" and you focused your search for answers on your career. This lead to the situation you find yourself in today. Did you include this situation in Question Two: Where to Start?

You may have:

➤ followed in your parents' footsteps and joined the same industry as your father or mother

➤ fought to do what you wanted to do against the wishes of your parents

➤ had parents, teachers, guidance counselors or managers who helped you discover and use your talents, or who advised and steered you in a specific direction so you realized your potential. You are in the minority.

You may be:

➤ doing what you are doing for a living by accident, not by plan. What may have started as a summer job when you were a teenager has become the career you find yourself in today. Would you let a teenager decide your future for you today?

➤ unhappy, but working for the money because you feel it is too late to change now

> ➤ lucky and are able to express your talents and follow your own interests in the job you are doing.

What do you want to do with the limited time you will be allowed to spend here on planet earth?

> *I asked an eight year old this question. After she had asked me to repeat the question, she promptly replied, "Have fun". How many grown-ups do you know who would come up with this answer? Do you know any grown-ups who would have any sort of answer?*
>
> —G. S. Cheesman

The grown-ups who asked you "What are you going to be when you grow up?" would have provided you with far more direction and more to think about if they had asked you this question instead: "What do you want to do with the limited time you will be allowed to spend here on planet earth?"

If this question had been imprinted on your brain and if you had relentlessly attempted to answer it, the focus of your whole life would have changed. Once you have chosen a set of goals for a balanced life, you will be well on your way to having the answer to this question.

How to find the right job for you

Whatever you label it—your occupation, your job, your career or your profession—the Role of paid or unpaid worker consumes more hours than any of your other roles throughout your life.

Right now, you could be in school or perhaps you are just starting to think about what your majors will be in university. You may be looking for a job or are thinking of changing jobs. Some of you are re-entering the work force, taking time off between jobs, transitioning to part-time work or are considering full - time retirement. Whatever your current situation is, you are thinking about your occupation and you are trying to decide what you are going to do next. You are planning to change how you spend the time of your life.

I developed the tool that follows to help you clarify what you want to do next.

MY IDEAL OCCUPATION

Write down all of the occupations you thought you might want to choose for yourself one day. Include what you have done before, or what you are doing now if you would choose it for yourself today. Don't list things you don't want to do again, unless you need to do this to find out why you found it unpleasant.

If you can remember, include from your youth, the answer to the question

"What are you going to be when you grow up?" Now ask yourself the new question "What do I want to do with the limited time I will be allowed to spend here on planet earth?"

List why each occupation appealed to you as a child—if it did. Now list why it appealed or appeals to you from your present perspective.

Is there anything that is "Fun" you can turn into your occupation? What will you do to occupy yourself? What did you always want to do? Is there something you really enjoyed doing in the past but you abandoned it because someone convinced you that it "didn't pay enough"?

Example:

Occupation	Why It Appealed to Me or Appeals to Me
Be a fireman, policeman	As a child: Wear a uniform with shiny buttons, have cars with lights and sirens
	As an adult: Serve and protect my community
Be a veterinarian	As a child: Heal sick animals, work with animals
	As an adult: Prevent pain and cruelty to animals
Be a rocket scientist	As a child: Launch rocket ships into space
	As an adult: Expand the body of knowledge of the universe

✓ REALITY CHECK

When you no longer need to earn, you still need to occupy your time—
what will you be doing then?

Write down all the ideas that occur to you – don't dismiss anything as "I couldn't do that now because". You are not eliminating options here in Part I of the book. Answer the question "Why it appeals or appealed to me" for inspiration on how to realize your ambition now.

Veterinarian
Why it appeals or appealed to me

➢ Heal sick animals, work with animals, prevent cruelty to animals

How can I do it now?

➢ Work or volunteer at the SPCA

➤ Become a part of the program to take animals to nursing homes to cheer the residents there

➤ Breed and sell my favorite breed of dog, cat or budgie.

Rocket Scientist
Why it appeals or appealed to me

➤ Launch rocket ships into space, expand the body of knowledge of the universe

How can I do it now?

➤ Join a model rocket club

➤ Start a toy company that specializes in model rockets

➤ Do tours at the planetarium.

Your imagination and creativity are the only limits. Ask for help from friends who know you well if you can't think of any possibilities. Making changes to your occupation requires courage. It involves a risk because you abandon the way you and other people view how you spend your time each day. You have to picture yourself in your new role. When you identify your Roadblocks in Part II, you can identify the Resources you have or need to acquire to overcome your Roadblocks.

When you are not paid to do the things you do, you may not call what you do work. Paid work is an exchange of your time, skills, knowledge and sometimes, your talents, for money. It is very easy to confuse the value of who you are as a person with the value in dollars you are earning. Unpaid work also uses your time, skills, knowledge and talents. The recipient, however, is not the only one who benefits. You receive internal rewards, such as a sense of accomplishment and the satisfaction of knowing you made a difference in someone's life.

✓ Reality Check

It is the time of your life you are spending.
Once it is gone, it is gone forever.

Socializing

When you want to have fun with other people, you turn to your family or you turn to people you have met through various social activities. You meet people who become your friends in your neighborhood, at school, through work or your community involvement with clubs, teams and organizations. Some of the people you meet remain as acquaintances; others become friends. All of the activities that are fun on your own are usually more fun with a favorite friend.

Giving Back to Society

When a need is unfilled, you can volunteer in your community. You occupy yourself as you use your time in the service of others. You usually end up having some fun, meeting new friends and it will be good for your soul. Volunteering is also a great way to broaden your network and gain skills to use for a paid occupation.

Getting out of the house and doing something for someone is a sure cure for depression and many other ills. Living in a community is not just about taking from it. To leave it a better place, you have to give something back. Become a part of the solution to the problem that "they" or "somebody" should do something about someday. Why not you?

Learning

Some of you consider yourselves a finished product and only learn something new by chance or when other people force you to. Choose to broaden your knowledge and dedicate yourself to lifelong learning. You continue to be interesting to others and interested in life. Organized learning offers you the opportunity to meet new people and to get out into your community. Learning on your own or with others is a great way to discover new talents and acquire new skills.

Clues to the subjects that interest you can be found by making a note of the following:

➤ What books and magazines do you read?

➤ What section of the newspaper do you turn to first?

➤ What is the subject of the TV shows you watch?

➤ What are the subjects of the news stories that get your attention?

➤ What stores do you go to?

➤ What section within a department or book store do you go to first?

If you had the time:

➤ What courses would you take?

➤ What organizations would you join?

➤ What seminars, classes or lectures would you attend?

➤ What languages would you learn?

➤ Where would you like to travel?

You have heard the expression "food for thought". Choose what you feed your mind.

Now that you have been introduced to the ten Keys to a Balanced Life, the examples that follow are here to help you classify your Someday lists—not as Activities you should include.

Example: Activities on your Someday lists classified under the ten Keys to a Balanced Life.

1   PHYSICAL HEALTH
Under the "Keys to a Balanced Life" column, enter "Physical Health". Under the "What I want to do" column, write down as many physical health Activities as you can think of, no matter how large, or how small.

➤ Run the Boston Marathon

➤ Walk one mile three days a week

➤ Play professional hockey, golf or basketball.

➤ Quit smoking.

2   MENTAL HEALTH
Under the "Keys to a Balanced Life" column, enter "Mental Health". Under the "What I want to do" column, write down as many mental health Activities as you can think of, no matter how large, or how small.

➤ Make setting and accomplishing my goals a priority for my life. Always know what I am going to do with the rest of my life.

➤ Develop an awareness of when I am being manipulated and act assertively (take an assertiveness course)

➤ Affirm to myself that whatever I do is good enough by my own standards

➤ Read self-awareness books.

3   MONEY
Under the "Keys to a Balanced Life" column, enter "Money". Under the "What I want to do" column, write down as many Activities as you can think of, no matter how large, or how small that you need money for. Your list might include some of these.

➤ Pay off my bills

➤ Take time off to do what I want to do

➤ Have a beautiful home in the country

➤ Pay for my children's college education.

4   FUN

Under the "Keys to a Balanced Life" column, enter "Fun". Under the "What I want to do" column, write down as many Activities as you can think of, no matter how large, or how small that you might want to do "just for fun". Examples were included under the description of this key.

5   GOOD FOR MY SOUL

Under the "Keys to a Balanced Life" column, enter "Good for my Soul". Under the "What I want to do" column, write down as many spirit renewing Activities as you can think of, no matter how large, or how small. What do you do that makes you say, "That was good for my soul". It could be:

➤ listen to an inspirational speaker tell a story of selfless sacrifice

➤ have a heart to heart talk with your best friend, spouse, mother, or child

➤ learn about the religions of the world

➤ worship with an organized congregation.

6   FAMILY

Under the "Keys to a Balanced Life" column, enter "Family". Under the "What I want to do" column, write down as many Activities as you can think of, no matter how large, or how small that you want to do with members of your family to fulfill your roles.

➤ vacation with my spouse to create memories together

➤ spend time with my grandchildren to be a part of their lives by teaching them to bake, camping with them, attending their concerts and sports days

➤ develop a romantic relationship to experience the joy of sharing my life with someone dear to me

➤ write a memoir of my experiences as a legacy for future generations to connect with their roots.

7   OCCUPATION

Under "Keys to a Balanced Life", write "Occupation". Write down every Activity you can think of, no matter how large or small, that you said you were going to do someday under "What I want to do". Include the occupations that you discovered using My Ideal Occupation tool.

If there is something you have always wanted to try—include it on your list. If you choose this Activity as your #1 Priority Activity to convert into a goal in Part II, at some point in your future you can then say, "I tried that and it turned out to be great or it turned out to be not for me". The alternative is to say, "I always wanted to do that someday" or "I had a chance to do that once, but I didn't do it; I don't know how it would have turned out".

✓ Reality Check

When you are in your rocking chair at the end of your life, you can say, "I tried that once and I have no regrets".

8   SOCIALIZING

Under "Keys to a Balanced Life", write "Socializing". Write down every Activity you can think of, no matter how large or small, that you said you were going to do someday for "What I want to do" to have fun or spend time with your family, friends, co-workers, fellow students or group members.

➤ See my friends on a regular basis

➤ Cruise to celebrate our 10th anniversary

➤ Go to a spa resort for a weekend of pampering

➤ Plan a monthly get together with schoolmates.

9   GIVING BACK TO SOCIETY

Under "Keys to a Balanced Life", write "Giving Back to Society". Write down every Activity you can think of, no matter how large or small, that you want to do to contribute to your community. You could:

➤ help service clubs and organizations

➤ participate in community organizations and events

➤ coach sports for children

➤ run for a political office.

10   LEARNING

Under "Keys to a Balanced Life", write "Learning". Write down every Activity you can think of, no matter how large or small, that you said you were going to do someday to learn something new either for personal satisfaction, or so you can change or advance in your occupation. As well as institutions of higher learning, night school and community centers offer opportunities to learn something new. Some of the things you might want to learn are:

➢ to speak Chinese

➢ how to program computers

➢ get a high school diploma or MBA

➢ how to woodwork to build things.

Learning can be fun; you can socialize; meet new friends; and perhaps do something for your physical health. Make a commitment to lifelong learning.

Exercise: Classify Your Someday Lists

The examples above are to help you classify your Someday lists not as Activities you should include.

For this exercise you need to think about, and write down, all the Activities that are important to you. Use the lists you have filed away somewhere or all those thoughts just floating around in your brain.

On your paper, your computer or in your notebook, write two headings, as follow. Using one page for each of the keys will make it easier to add Activities as you think of them.

Keys to a Balanced Life   **What I want to do**
                               Activities from my Someday list

Do these in any order you'd like. Perhaps one area of your life is out of balance right now and you want to focus on it first. Maybe you are curious to find out how you feel or what you want to do in one particular key because you haven't really thought about it before. This can be a journey of self-discovery as you find out where your current priorities lie.

You are listing these Activities. You are not doing these things first. These are Activities, not Goals. What does matter is to list every Activity on your Someday lists under the key that seems to fit it best.

Once you have done that, try to come up with at least one Activity under each of the keys. If you don't at first, re-read the preceding examples and do some thinking on your own. It won't be long before you have your own Someday list under each of the keys.

List all the Activities that you would like to do someday, either from your Someday list or by making a note of ideas for activities as they occur to you.

Another name for just listing things as they occur to you is brainstorming. When you brainstorm you do not edit or call anything impossible. You are making a list—ideas you will prioritize and evaluate using the Decision Process in Part II.

BRAINSTORMING

It amazes me how often a brainstorming session is held to address a business issue, with experienced professionals in attendance who use their valuable time to come up with a list of potential activities to address the issue and then no one follows through.

Needless to say, these initiatives fail to achieve the desired results. The person who initiated the brainstorming session does not convert the ideas into goals.

This not only represents a huge potential opportunity cost for the company but it also discourages the attendees because they were asked for input which was then ignored.

The ideas resulting from any brainstorming session are only that—ideas, activities, or things to do. The Eight-Step Decision Process must be applied to the list of activities resulting from any brainstorming to convert them into achievable goals.

QUESTION FIVE:

Do you have the time?

Invest your time—don't just spend it.
—G. S. Cheesman

When you spend all your money, you are broke. When you spend all your time, well the fact is, you are dead. The difference, of course, is that you can do a cash flow and figure out when you are going to run out of money, make a plan to earn more or cut your expenses.

With time—there is no telling when you are going to run out of that. Because we, as a society need to measure things, time is measured with clocks and calendars. You can use the time you have to do the things that are important to you—or to do nothing at all. The decision is yours. In this section you learn about your irreplaceable resource, time.

➤ The Myths of Time

➤ Time Facts

➤ The Time of Your Life

➤ The Time Shortfall

➤ Trade-offs

The Myths of Time

Time can't be saved for a rainy day. There is really no such thing as spare time or free time. You can't have time on your hands or kill time. If you say you are killing time, you are misusing the most valuable resource of your life.

Time Facts

Each day has 24 hours. Each year, except a Leap Year, has 365 days.

✔ REALITY CHECK

Every person, without exception,
has 8760 hours each year to spend — no more!

You need to have an idea of how you are spending the time of your life. At least once a year, you need to record where your time is going. Recording how you spend your time is a time-consuming Activity. Do you have any idea of how you are spending your time?

When you defined what goal setting meant to you, you committed to adding the Activity of Goal Setting to your life. Activities take time, but every Activity is a reflection of a goal. Your definition clarifies what goal setting means to you. When you have completed the exercises in this book, you will know what goals are driving your Activities.

The Time of Your Life

In Question Three, you identified each of your roles. In the exercise that follows, you will write down the Activities you do in each of your roles and an estimate of the time you spend doing those Activities. If you don't feel you can make guesses about how much time you spend doing the things you do, you can keep track of where and how you spend your time on a daily basis.

Pick a normal (for you) two-week period to observe and record your behavior. Write down the Activities for each of your roles. After a few days, you will start to see a pattern emerge.

The time you are recording is not how much time you feel you should spend, but the actual time you do spend being busy with these Activities. Appendix A illustrates a detailed example entitled "The Time of Your Life".

✔ REALITY CHECK

For each Activity you choose to do,
there is a price in the amount of time that must be planned for it
and the cost of giving up other Activities.

As you record how you spend your time, you might find it helpful to write down the Activity first, and then make a note every time you do that Activity in a day.

Example:

Activity: Phone Calls

➤ Less than a minute Dentist's office reminding me of my appointment

➤ 15 minutes Mother to remind me to come for dinner Saturday and we talked of other things

➤ 35 minutes Cousin to catch up on family news.

At the end of the day, add up the minutes you spent on the phone and divide by 60 to get the number of hours. At work, interruptions tend to be the rule, not the exception. For this exercise, note the hours you devote to the Activity of work, not the Activities at work—that is a whole other exercise.

Once you have an estimate, or a detailed record, of how you spent your time during a "normal for you" two-week period, you can multiply by 26. You arrive at an approximate number of hours you spend each year on each Activity.

Note: Each year has 52 weeks, plus one day. 52 weeks times 7 days equals 364 days. 364 days times 24 hours per day equals 8736 hours, plus one 24-hour day equals 8760 hours available to you in one non-Leap Year.

As you record the Activities you do in each of your roles, keep track of the declining balance as you use the 8760 hours available to you in a year. Subtract the total annual time you use for your first Activity from 8760. Subtract the annual time for the next Activity from the remaining hours.

If you wish to make an allowance for your vacation time when you would suspend your normal activities, subtract your vacation days from 365. Multiply your normal days times 24 to arrive at the number of hours you want to use instead of 8760. Use your unique formula.

The example that follows uses a grid to record the time you could spend doing various Activities in one of your roles. You can use your computer, pad of paper, notebook or whatever works for you. If you have more than one child, you would name your children as you noted the Activities you do in your Role of Parent.

Example: Recording the time you spend doing various Activities in your roles

Family Role: Mother / Father Relationship with Child.

Activities To maintain this relationship	Hours	Time Spent Per Day	Total Annual Time Spent on this Activity	8760 MINUS Annual Time Spent
E-mail Child	7:00am–7:15am 3 times per week	Quarter hour or .25 hours	3 times X .25 hour X 50 weeks per year= 37.5	37.5 from 8760 = 8722.5
Play Golf With Child	6:00am– 2:00pm One time per month	8 hours	12 months X 8 hours = 96	8722.5 minus 96 = 8626.5
Attend seminar with Child once every quarter	7:00pm– 9:00pm plus dinner – 6:00pm– 7:00pm plus travel 5:30pm–6:00pm and 9:00pm – 9:30pm	4 hours	4 quarters in one year X 4 hours = 16	8626.5 minus 16 = 8610.5
			37.5 plus 96 plus 16 = 149.5 hours	8760 minus 149.5 = 8610.5

Exercise: The Time of Your Life

Record the time you spend doing the various Activities in your roles.

Refer to the examples above and in Appendix A.

The Time Shortfall

The brutal reality of life is that there isn't enough time to do everything. The other reality is that unless you consciously recognize this, one year slips into the next. Things you wanted to do this year are moved forward into next year, or become part of your Someday list because you ran out of time. In Part II, you will learn All About Priorities.

If you haven't already done so, refer to Appendix A. Are you surprised? Annoyed? Frustrated? Even with the modest estimates that were used for many of the Activities, you would need to find over 48 hours each and every week to do all of the listed Activities. Here are just a few examples of where the time goes.

Examples from Appendix A:

➤ When you look at the Activity of cooking, you can see why restaurant meals, fast food, take out and home delivery are so popular – 700 hours over 50 work weeks is 14 hours per week, or two hours per day just to prepare food. (Subtract meals at work)

➤ Add another 350 hours to do dishes, or seven hours per week for 50 work weeks, and then add the one hour per week to grocery shop, not including travel time and time to put the groceries away. (Subtract meals at work)

➤ Over the time frame of 50 work weeks, 14 hours of TV watching a week, is only two hours per day, but adds up to 700 hours in a year, and this doesn't include web-surfing on your computer as a potential substitute for TV time.

➤ One-half hour per day devoted exclusively to your spousal equivalent costs another three and a half hours per week, or only 175 hours per year.

Trade-offs

Trade-offs exist whenever you choose to spend your time in one Role engaging in one Activity instead of another. Trade-offs exist when you acquire possessions that then have to be insured and maintained, costing you time and money.

Develop an awareness of the choices you make. They all involve trade-offs in the use of your irreplaceable resource—time.

✓ REALITY CHECK

The secret to having enough time to do everything you want to do
is to narrow down what you want to do
by establishing your #1 Priority Activities.

You have now completed Part I, the information search for problem solving process. You have your answers to:

Question One: What is goal setting?

How you define goal setting.

Question Two: Where to start?

    The information about where you are today.

Question Three: Who are you? Role Call

    A list of your roles.

Question Four: How do you balance your life?

    Your Someday lists classified under each of the ten Keys to a Balanced Life.

Question Five: Do you have the time?

    Where you are spending the time of your life.

You are now ready to use the Eight–Step Decision Process to create a set of goals that reflects who you are, what you want to do and the life you want for yourself.

PART II
PUTTING THE GO
INTO GOAL SETTING

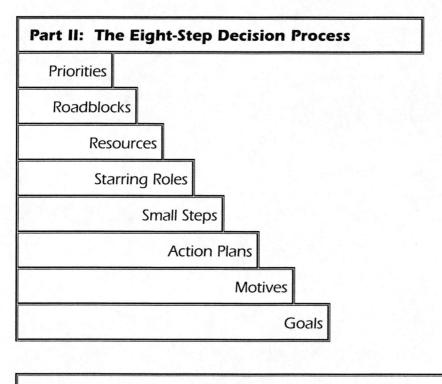

Part II: The Eight-Step Decision Process

Priorities

Roadblocks

Resources

Starring Roles

Small Steps

Action Plans

Motives

Goals

Mission in Life

Appendix B has examples of the Eight-Step Decision Process from two perspectives.

One example starts with Activities and builds up to the source of those Activities —Your Mission in Life.

The other example starts with a Goal that reflects your Mission in Life and then breaks down into the Activities you focus on to accomplish the Goal.

STEP ONE:

All About Priorities

Priority Activities ➜ Roadblocks ➜ Resources

➜ Roles ➜ Small Steps ➜ Action Plans ➜

Motives ➜ Goals ➜ Mission

In Part I, you listed everything you ever wanted to do someday for each of the ten keys. Because you were brainstorming, and not calling anything impossible, you have long lists of Activities under each of the keys. This section covers:

- Two methods of choosing priorities
- Conflicting priorities
- Switching priorities
- Shifting between priorities
- Using 10 percent of your time to change your life
- Changing Someday lists into One Day lists

✓ REALITY CHECK

You do not have unlimited Resources.
Time alone limits the options
you can undertake and accomplish.

Choosing, then single-mindedly focusing on one Activity is extremely difficult. Keep your #1 Priority Activity as your priority until you have converted it into a goal. If an attractive option comes along, list this Activity under the appropriate key for action someday. Once you have recorded it, forget it for now.

Exercise: Part I: Two Methods of Choosing Priorities

#1 Priorities can be identified from all your possible activities, and decided by:

1) Asking yourself:

> ➤ "If I could do only one of these in my lifetime, which one would it be?"

> ➤ "If I had twenty million dollars, which one of these would I still want to do?"

> ➤ "If I had one wish, what would it be?"

If any of these work for you, write a #1 beside that Activity and work through all of the keys until you have chosen one #1 Priority for each.

2) Checks and X's:

One	For each of the ten keys, number the Activities you have listed.
Two	Ask yourself, "If I could only do #1 and I would have to give up, for now, #2, #3, #4, #5 etc, would I choose #1 as my first priority?"
Three	If the answer is No, make an X beside it. Move to #2.
Four	If the answer is Yes, make a check beside it. Move to #2.
Five	Ask yourself, "If I could only do #2 and not #1, #3, #4, #5 etc, would I choose #2?"
Six	Again, attach a check or an X to #2 and move on to #3.

To evaluate the rest of your Activities, repeat the procedure for all of the Activities on your lists.

If you have more than one Activity with a check beside it, create a new list of these Activities. Repeat steps One to Six until you have only one Activity for each key with a check beside it. You have now chosen a #1 Priority Activity for each of the ten keys. The rest of your Activities are on hold for now.

Conflicting Priorities

Your ten #1 Priority Activities create a list that represents the Activities you have chosen to change into goals. Ask yourself, "**Do they fit together?**" Your list might look like this:

Physical Health

1   Develop a lifestyle that includes exercise to increase my physical well-being, energy level and mental alertness.

Mental Health

1   Read self-awareness books.

Occupation

1   Take a year off to be a painter.

Family

1   Start a family and stay at home.

Fun

1   Go to an art gallery.

Good for My Soul

1   Read inspirational books and poems.

Socializing

1   Schedule time with my friends.

Giving Back to Society

1   Work with children at schools and hospitals.

Learning

1   Take a course in painting with watercolors.

Money

1   Buy a bigger home in the country.

Fit versus Conflict

Before you change your #1 Priority Activities into goals, you want to ensure that they fit together and are not conflicting priorities. Your priorities must be consistent and support one another.

Example: Identify Conflicting Priorities

Your Occupational #1 Priority of quitting your job to take a year off to be a portrait painter is going to present you with challenging Roadblocks if your Money priority is to buy a bigger home in the country and your Family priority is to stay at home because you plan to start a family.

Buying a large country home with equally large mortgage payments is going to present a major source of conflict with your priority of quitting your job which conflicts with your desire to paint and to start a family.

It is not impossible to mesh these priorities, but it definitely increases the Resources you need for their accomplishment.

✓ REALITY CHECK

If you focus on a different priority,
you are going to get different results.

The following example is a partial list of priority Activities that fit together.

Example: Activities that fit together

Occupation. Take a year off to paint.
Keep my job for the next year. Work toward establishing myself as a painter in my non–work time.
Family. Start a family.
This is a minimum of nine months.
Money. Buy a house in the country.
Add a year to my planning horizon. Make this a priority for two years from now. Continue to save for the down payment. The mortgage I will need won't be as large.

Exercise: Part II: Identify Conflicting Priorities

Look for any conflicts among your #1 Priority Activities. If conflicts exist, they represent Roadblocks you have to overcome. Roadblocks are presented in detail in the next section.

Switching Priorities

Choose priorities that can be successfully accomplished using a variety of Resources. Do not depend on the availability of a single Resource to accomplish all of your priorities. The more Roadblocks you face, the more Resources you need to overcome them. If you have too many Roadblocks and you don't have enough Resources, consider abandoning this #1 Priority for now, not indefinitely, just this time around.

✓ REALITY CHECK

Your priorities must be consistent and support one another;
this makes it possible to seamlessly weave them together.

If you have conflicting priorities, you require more Resources to overcome the Roadblocks you encounter, and you still may be unable to make them fit together.

Exercise: Part III: Switching Priorities to Avoid Conflicts

Go back and look at what else you can do. Would it be more reasonable and realistic to trade-off an Activity that is causing a conflict and choose another Activity instead if it is a better fit?

By working on a #1 Priority Activity for each of the ten keys, you establish balance in your life. Having balance in your life is an enormously freeing experience. It makes it clear which activities you can do now, which to ignore until later, and the certainty that you are accomplishing the things that are important to you.

✓ REALITY CHECK

Devote some time each day to developing every one of your
ten #1 Priority Activities into Goals.

Shifting between Priorities

In a perfectly balanced life, you would devote an equal amount of time to each of your ten priorities every day. As you might have found when you completed the time use exercise, some roles need more time.

Example: Shifting between Priorities

Each week, devote one hour and forty-five minutes to your #1 Priority Activity for the Key of Learning (15 minutes times 7 days).

If you have decided that 1:00pm to 1:30pm is the best time to make progress on this priority, set aside this time on Tuesday, Thursday and Sunday, and 15 minutes on

Saturday. Total one hour and forty-five minutes.

At 12:55pm, on Sunday, the phone rings. Your Socializing #1 Priority demands your attention.

You have to make a decision. If you Socialize at this time instead of Learning, is it going to work out best for you? Are the time slots for these two priorities interchangeable? When will you re-allocate the time to Learning? If you can resolve these questions to your satisfaction, and you decide it is worth it to you to shift priorities on this occasion, then do it.

Don't get caught in the time-slip trap. Time-slip occurs when you try to play catch-up by moving the time into the next week, next month, or even next year.

If you find Socializing frequently replaces your other #1 Priority Activities, revisit your list of ten priorities. Confirm that Socializing is a priority for you, and not a way to procrastinate or to meet other people's priorities. Remind yourself that you have committed to your other nine priorities as well.

Exercise: Part IV: Block Time on Your Calendar

Decide when you are going to block time daily or weekly to work on your priorities. Devote time to a priority Activity for each key to achieve balance in your life.

✔ REALITY CHECK

You have 24 hours in each day,
the same as everyone else on the planet.
You choose how to spend those hours.

Just knowing you have more than one priority increases your desire to attempt to introduce balance into your life. Try to balance your life as best as you can.

Your 10 Percent Investment

Once you have chosen your priorities, block fifteen minutes each day, at a minimum, to devote to each. Fifteen minutes each day, every day of the year is 5475 minutes or 91.25 hours each year. Fifteen minutes each day is a total of two hours and thirty minutes per day for all ten priorities. This is less than ten percent of the hours available to you in a day but the payoff will be much greater when you experience the difference in your life.

✓ REALITY CHECK

*If you can't find two hours and thirty minutes each day to devote to
what you have said are your life priorities,
you are randomly going with the flow.*

*You are in danger of running out of time and
finding yourself at the end of your life with regrets for the things you
didn't do or didn't even try.*

In Step Five: Take Small Steps, you identify actions to move your Activities toward becoming Goals. Plan your small steps to fit into the fifteen-minute blocks of time you set aside daily for each priority. Include them on your daily To Do list.

It is not the quantity of time you allocate, but the quality of the time. By designating even fifteen minutes a day exclusively to each of your priorities, without interruptions or distractions, you devote your best time to the Activities that are most important to you.

Small things can make a big difference

By working with Priorities, you make a conscious decision to do the things that are important to you. If a daily time schedule doesn't seem feasible to you, allocate the time on a weekly basis.

Exercise: Part V: A Weekly Schedule

Each week, schedule one hour and forty-five minutes for each of the ten keys. Your week has seven days, each with 24 hours for a total of 168 hours. You decide at what points during the week you are going to work on each of your priorities.

✓ REALITY CHECK

*At a minimum, commit
one and three-quarter hours to each of your priorities during the week.
This is a total of seventeen and one-half hours per week.
You still have over 150 hours to schedule as you choose.
How will you spend your time?*

Leave It Out

You may find it helpful to find a place where you can leave your project out. If you exercise, it is easier if you have your treadmill or weight bench in a convenient spot. If you paint, it is easier to get back to it if your easel is set up. If you woodwork, it is easier if your tools and materials can be left in place.

If your Activity is Goal Setting, it is easier if this book, your notebook, your pens, pencils and calculator have "a place to live" where you see them and work with them on a daily basis.

Exercise: Part VI: Organize Your Project Space

Find one drawer, shelf or cupboard and designate it as your project space. Place all of your supplies into one basket or box. Maybe you want to have ten containers, or file folders, one for your notes on each of your ten #1 Priority Activities. This way you can get right to it instead of having to add time to get everything together and then to put everything away.

Eventually, your daily or weekly time commitments expand to the point where the majority of your time is totally devoted to your priorities. At the very least, you will approach each day with the awareness that you have priorities in the ten key areas of life.

Be Aware

As you practice devoting time to your priorities, you develop an awareness of when you are, and when you aren't, actually making progress toward accomplishing what you have said is important to you.

When you are aware of what you are doing, you can consciously and thoughtfully choose activities that contribute to your priorities. This helps you to gain a sense of accomplishment, contentment and balance in your life.

Example: How an Activity can be a part of your Mission in Life

Activity: Playing ball in the backyard with your children or grandchildren.

Role: Parent / Grandparent.

Key to a Balanced Life: Family.
  #1 Priority Activity: Being a part of my children's / grandchildren's lives.

Key to a Balanced Life: Fun / Socializing
  #1 Priority Activity: Play a sport (ball).

Goal*:* My vision is to create a nurturing and supportive environment for my family wherever they are around the world.

Mission in Life: *I will do my utmost to raise children that are contributing members of society.*

Mission in Life: *I will ensure those I love know that I love them, by my actions first, and then my words.*

Exercise: Part VII: Developing Awareness

Ask the following questions periodically throughout the day. You may be surprised and pleased by the answers.

➢ What Role am I in right now?

➢ Which of the ten Keys to a Balanced Life would this Activity fall under?

➢ Is this Activity one of the small steps I have included as a way of accomplishing one of my goals?

If you feel you are giving up too much freedom and flexibility by scheduling time for these Activities, you might want to abandon this process – don't! You chose these ten #1 Priority Activities and you decided they were the most important things to you.

If your life was extremely out of balance, it will be difficult, but not impossible, to refocus. Dedicate at least fifteen minutes a day to each priority. This will feel like less of a change than finding one hour and forty-five minutes weekly.

Your Someday Lists are Now One Day Lists

Establishing priorities is a time-consuming, but necessary, project because it clarifies where your true priorities lie at the moment. It also focuses your time—your most valuable resource—on ten #1 Priorities.

Keep the Someday lists you worked from when you classified your "things I want to do someday" into the Keys to a Balanced Life. The good news is that you will accomplish your #1 Priority as you use the Eight-Step Decision Process to convert your Activities into your Goals.

You will then choose a new #1 Priority Activity from your Someday list. For each of the ten keys, you had a #2 Priority Activity. Possibly, you will choose this Activity as your new priority. If your priorities have changed, you may feel another Activity from that key is more deserving of your time and attention next.

If your ten #1 Priority Activities have been on your Someday list for quite some time, you need to find out what the Roadblocks are that have been keeping them there.

STEP TWO:

Identify Your Roadblocks

Priority Activities ➔ **Roadblocks** ➔ Resources

➔ Roles ➔ Small Steps ➔ Action Plans

➔ Motives ➔ Goals ➔ Mission

A construction Roadblock stops you temporarily. It may be in place for weeks or for months. If it is in place for any length of time, you find a different route, rather than deal with the detour on a daily basis.

There are Roadblocks, real or imagined, that have kept you from doing the things you have said you want to do. Until you identify them, they continue to have the power to stop you. You victimize yourself without knowing what the problem is. This section will cover:

- A List of Potential Roadblocks
- How Other People's Priorities are a Roadblock
- Measures
- Labels
- Detours

Once you identify the Roadblocks that keep you from doing what you want to do, focus on finding or developing the Resources to overcome them. Be really honest with yourself. Verify that you are working on the problem, not a symptom of the problem.

✓ REALITY CHECK

A problem is like an iceberg,
one-tenth in full view, and nine-tenths hidden.
What appears to be the problem could just be the tip of the iceberg.

A List of Potential Roadblocks

➤ **Your Critic**
The way the little voice in your head talks to you. "I can't".

➤ **Your Secret Fears**
The secret fears only you know and that are probably imaginary.

➤ **Your Perception of Your Physical Appearance and Abilities**
Your body shape, your height, your state of health, your physical ability

➤ **Your Perception of Your Skill Level**
Competence, experience, confidence, education

➤ **Your View of Your Natural Endowments**
Talents, intelligence, musical or artistic ability, sense of humor

➤ **Your Current Financial Status**
Over committed, working, unemployed

➤ **Your Lifestyle Status**
Your age, sex, marital status, being a parent

➤ **Other People's Opinions and Priorities**.

Other People

You encounter other people in all of your Interactive Roles. Other People's opinions of you and what you are doing can prevent you from doing what you want to do. The need to impress other people, the need to prove something to yourself or to the world can be a Roadblock to your progress.

Other People's Priorities. Strained Encounters

In Part I, you looked at where you are today and you decided if some of the situations were in response to other people's priorities.

You encounter other people as you work on your #1 Priority Activities. Other people and their demands are frequently Roadblocks to the achievement of your goals.

Many of these demands don't seem like demands, especially when they are worded as requests. Other people and their demands are difficult to ignore, because they are the people you love, respect or fear. Their control over your emotions can sway you from your best intentions to focus on your priority Activities. No is a hard word to say. Especially at home and at work, you will be faced with a conflict between other people's priorities and your priorities. It is hard to say no to a loved one, but it's harder to say no at work.

Other People at Work

Company owners, or people they hire, formulate goals and choose strategies to achieve these goals. These strategies are formed at various levels within the business and are based on the priorities of the individuals involved. They are then communicated down the organization to managers who have been hired to implement them.

The individual manager establishes goals to achieve the strategies that have been formed higher up in the organization. The manager's role is to use the people who have been hired as employees to achieve his goals, which in turn achieve the goals of the company's owner.

Much of the time this is where the goal setting process stops. The employees are told what to do, usually through job descriptions and on-the-job training. They are the human resources that the manager uses, or uses up, to accomplish his goals.

When you work for someone's company, you have chosen to include their priorities as part of your priorities. If you can limit your time involvement in their priorities, and not place their priorities before your priorities, you have a better chance of achieving balance in your life.

You have your own list of reasons why (Roadblocks) you haven't been able to do what you want to do up until now. You are not alone. The following section on Measures and Labels illustrates other ways you compare yourself to Other People.

How Are You Doing? Measures and Labels

Measuring and labeling starts when you are born: boy / girl, time and date you were born, name, length, weight. Then your parents schedule when you will be fed, changed and when you will sleep. Fortunately, you are blissfully unaware that all this is going on. Later, in the terrible two's you start to make your opinion known when you discover the word "No".

The difference between a measure and a label is that an accurate measure returns the same result each time you use it. Labels are subjective and change depending on who is doing the labeling.

Measures

Humans are competitive. Each society has developed a complex set of measures to determine who is the best in a particular area at a specific point in time.

➤ Which markers or milestones do you use to evaluate your progress? Physical or Mental? External or Internal? Objective or Subjective?

➤ Do you compare yourself against an external standard? Is it an accurate measure of what you want to accomplish?

➢ Is the measuring tool you are using accurate? Is it giving you the answers to the questions you have?

➢ Are you asking the right questions?

Societies measure and compare people and everything they do. Be aware of when and how you are measuring yourself and your progress.

The society you live in sends you messages to tell you how to measure your progress, to know how you are doing and when "you have arrived". The problem is that society keeps moving the finish line. Having your own goals lets you control where the finish line is.

External Measures

Here are some of the external measures you are told you can use to measure your progress against some other person, class of people, or situation.

External Measures

➢ Dollars and the material things that dollars buy are used to compare social standing, as well as actual wealth.

● Clothes, shoes, jewelry

● Car, boat, plane

● House, villa, mansion

● Vacations in exotic locations.

➢ Pictorial Representations

● Graphs are used to find out who is average, and to track the progress of someone or something

○ Direction – up or down by how much or what percentage

● Blueprints/Maps tell you how far you've come, how far you have to go, and how the end result should look.

➢ Mechanical Measures

● Gauges - Fluid – empty/full, Speed – fast/slow, mph/kph

● Clocks & Calendars - minutes, hours, deadlines/schedules, days/weeks/months/years.

➢ Conceptual Measures

   ● Report Cards - grades /marks, IQ's

   ● Scores - runs, touchdowns, goals.

Labels

Subjective measures are somebody's opinion. It could be your opinion or somebody else's opinion. This is labeling because not everyone would feel the same way. A label is a descriptive or identifying term. In Part I, how you see yourself is a label called "Your Roles".

Labels

➢ State of Being

   ● Happy / Unhappy

   ● Attractive / Unattractive

   ● Relaxed / Stressed

   ● Good / Bad

   ● Rich / Poor

➢ How you see yourself physically

   ● Fat/Thin

   ● Tall/Short

➢ Many of the Roadblocks & Resources you list are labels

➢ Every one of your Roles is a label.

There are unlimited lists of measures and labels you can use to judge your position in, and progress against, the rest of your society. Ignoring the messages that are constantly bombarding you is extremely difficult to do, but it can be done if you are aware of them.

   Just for fun, record the messages that you see or hear when you are reading a magazine or watching TV for just one evening. What external things are you being asked to worry about? If you classified these messages under the ten keys, which keys would they fall under?

   Internal, instead of external direction, puts the control of your life firmly into your hands because internal labels are Resources.

Detours

Detours are sometimes necessary to avoid a bad patch of road, but it is best to avoid them if at all possible. Detours slow you down and sidetrack you from your chosen path. You arrive at your destination eventually as long as you have sufficient Resources to get you there.

You may detour off your chosen path if the Roadblocks you identified for your #1 Priority are just too numerous. Choose a different route. Consider choosing your #2 Priority as your first choice for this key.

You may have too many Roadblocks and too few Resources. If you find yourself in this situation, try to eliminate the Roadblocks and add to your Resources as you work on another Activity. This increases your ability to successfully tackle your original priority.

Example: Roadblocks

➢ My attitude, I can't because I'm not physical enough, skilled enough, knowledgeable enough, talented enough, I don't deserve success

➢ Too old

➢ Too busy, I don't have time

➢ Too lazy, too comfortable with the way things are

➢ Requires too much work to change

➢ I have to work to pay my bills, I don't have the money

➢ Procrastination, I'll do it later

➢ I'd have to go back to school, I don't have the education

➢ I don't know how to do that, I've never done it before

➢ I'm not any good at that

➢ I tried that once and it didn't work

➢ I don't have the equipment or tools to do the job

➢ Other People – Family, Friends, I'll look foolish; everyone will laugh at me, what if I fail?

Exercise: Roadblocks

➤ Transfer each of your ten #1 Priority Activities to a separate sheet of paper, divided into four columns with headings as follows.

Key to a Balanced Life, My #1 Priority Activity, Roadblocks, Resources

➤ For each of your #1 Priority Activities, list any of the preceding, or any of your own, reasons why you have not or could not accomplish it.

STEP THREE:

Apply Your Resources

Priority Activities ➜ Roadblocks ➜ **Resources**

➜ Roles ➜ Small Steps ➜ Action Plans

➜ Motives ➜ Goals ➜ Mission

Your Roadblocks have to be eliminated with Resources. The irreplaceable resource you are definitely going to run out of is time. How you choose to allocate your Resources is under your control. It doesn't matter if you don't have the Resources now; just identify the ones you need. You can decide later which Resources you can or want to acquire. This section covers:

- Internal Labels
- A List of Potential Resources

Inner Strength

Internal labels are labels you choose to apply to yourself. They include your:

➢ attitude, especially towards others

➢ outlook toward circumstances

➢ values

➢ conduct

➢ use of your time.

A partial list of internal labels follows.

Internal Labels

➢ Your attitude, especially towards others

- Cheerful   Glum
- Cooperative   Obstructive
- Willing   Unwilling

- Supportive   Critical
- Tolerant   Judgmental
- Equitable   Bully
- Fair   Oppressive
- Respectful   Disrespectful.

➤ Your outlook toward circumstances

- Positive   Negative
- Abundance   Scarcity
- Optimistic   Pessimistic
- Act   Procrastinate
- Change   Permanence
- Progressive   Out of date
- Courageous   Fearful
- Secure   Insecure.

➤ Your values

- Truth   Deceit
- Justice   Injustice
- Dignity   Scorn
- Integrity   Dishonorable
- Honest   Dishonest
- Knowledge   Ignorance
- Punctuality   Tardiness.

➤ Your conduct

- Class   Crass
- Consistent   Contradictory
- Energetic   Lazy
- Disciplined   Undisciplined
- Pleasant, Nice   Horrible, loud and obnoxious
- Ethical   Unethical
- Loyal   Disloyal.

➢ You control your time

- ● Where you spend your time
- ● Who you spend your time with
- ● How you spend your time
- ● What you spend your time doing
- ● When you spend time
- ● Why you spend time.

You control the elements of your personality and character. Use these internal labels when you measure yourself and your progress.

Resources

The number of Resources you have, or that you can acquire, includes everything you can creatively think of as a way to overcome a Roadblock. A partial list of Resources follows.

A LIST OF POTENTIAL RESOURCES

➢ **Time**
Your attitude toward it

➢ **Self-discipline**
Relentlessly applying yourself to your priorities

➢ **Education**
The Three R's – reading, writing and arithmetic and specialized knowledge

➢ **Skills**
Things you have learned how to do

➢ **Talents**
Things you do naturally all the time

➢ **Physical ability**
Coordination, strength, speed

➢ **Courage**
The bravery to live your way

➢ **Risk taking**
Considering yourself your best bet

➢ **Equipment**
The tools needed for the job

➤ **Self-esteem**
   Your good opinion of yourself

➤ **Money**
   What you need money for and knowing how much is enough

➤ **Confidence**
   Your belief in yourself independent of anyone else's opinion

➤ **Experience**
   You have done it before; you can do it again – only better

➤ **People**
   Having someone believe in you. Your family, your friends, your network, your support group.

Your Support Group

Having a circle of friends or people with similar interests to meet with on a regular basis is a useful resource to develop. Choose people who encourage you and help you to overcome procrastination, and who will be a source of fresh ideas when you get stuck in a rut. These are Other People who have opinions that you value, but the choice is still yours whether you embrace their ideas or reject them.

✔ REALITY CHECK

*If the Roadblocks for each of
your #1 Priority Activities are the same,
recognize that the same Resources
are required to eliminate those Roadblocks.*

Exercise: Apply Your Resources

For each of your Roadblocks, list the Resources you have. List the Resources you can acquire.

Your Resources are limited. You know what can stop you from accomplishing your #1 Priority Activities—Roadblocks. You know how to eliminate the Roadblocks— apply Resources. Next, you will match your roles to your Priorities.

STEP FOUR:

In the Starring Role

Priority Activities ➔ Roadblocks ➔ Resources

➔ **Roles** ➔ Small Steps ➔ Action Plans

➔ Motives ➔ Goals ➔ Mission

To achieve balance in your life, you need to devote time to all ten keys. You have selected a #1 Priority Activity for each of the keys. Each Activity is done in one of your roles. In this section, you will:

- Match your roles with the Keys to a Balanced Life
- Identify your Dominant Roles
- Learn how roles and the Keys to a Balanced Life work together

Example: Roles attached to a partial list of #1 Priority Activities

➢ Key: Occupation
- Role: Worker   Be a painter

➢ Key: Money
- Role: Romantic Partner   Buy a house in the country

➢ Key: Socializing
- Role: Friend   Schedule time with my friends

➢ Key: Family
- Role: Romantic Partner   Start a family

➢ Key: Giving Back to Society
- Role: Volunteer   Work with children at schools

➢ Key: Physical Health
- Role: Individual   Develop a lifestyle that includes exercise to increase my physical well-being and energy level.

✓ Reality Check

Activities keep you busy; goals achieve results.

Exercise: Attach Your Roles

Add another column next to Resources and list your roles for each of your #1 Priority Activities.

Key to a Balanced Life, #1 Priority Activity, Roadblocks, Resources, Roles.

Role I will be in when I start this Activity _____.

You have now attached roles to each of your #1 Priorities. Are you using one of your roles to accomplish several of your priorities? If you are, this is one of your Dominant Roles.

What are Your Dominant Roles?

All of you have two or three roles that feel *really* comfortable. Some of you refer to this as your "comfort zone". These Dominant Roles define how you think of yourself and are your preferred way of presenting yourself to the world.

A Dominant Role can be identified by:

➤ Where you spent the majority of your time according to your Time Use Total.

➤ Who you think you are when you get up on Saturday morning or whatever your day off is. Mother, lover, daughter, worker?

➤ Who you are working for:

- Parent – your child / children – their future, their education
- Daughter / Son – to pay for a nursing home
- Individual
  - ○ Your Lifestyle
  - ○ House
  - ○ Car
  - ○ Entertainment
  - ○ Your Future Lifestyle
  - ○ Retirement

➤ Where do you spend your thought energy? Wishing you were doing something else? Thinking about your spouse, thinking or worrying about your job, worrying about your future, thinking about your parents, fretting about your children?

Exercise: Identify Your Dominant Roles

Highlight, check or circle the three roles where you spend most of your time from the roles that you attached to your #1 Priority Activities. Depending on your age and life-stage, the role of worker or student/learner always demands a specific time commitment, a surrendering of control over time. The question is whether or not you allow the time commitment to become excessive, and you neglect your other roles and relationships.

You have one key that you say is your priority. Often, it will be family. Is this where you spend the majority of your time? If you feel you are working for your family—to provide for them—is there a way you could provide less material objects and more of your time? Is your priority in the top three roles you just highlighted?

In the next section, you will identify the small steps you need to take to successfully achieve your #1 Priority Activities.

STEP FIVE:

Take Small Steps

Priority Activities ➔ Roadblocks ➔ Resources

➔ Roles ➔ **Small Steps** ➔ Action Plans

➔ Motives ➔ Goals ➔ Mission

Just as you can't lose ten pounds by noon tomorrow, each Activity has small steps you can take to move it toward becoming a goal that you can achieve. These small steps are actions you identify to break a vague Activity into specific steps. They spell out what it is you need to do in small, manageable steps suited to your roadblocks and resources. This section covers:

- Seeking Inspiration
- What small steps look like
- How small steps increase your Resources

Seeking Inspiration

If you can't seem to see possible actions for a particular priority activity:

➢ move on to another key. One sometimes inspires ideas for another.

➢ ask a friend what he would do. Find out if he has solutions that will work for you.

➢ seek expert advice

➢ read a book

➢ look on the Internet

➢ take a course

➢ find someone who has done what you are trying to do. What lessons has he learned that you can benefit from?

➢ brainstorm to come up with a list of possible ideas, either by yourself or with someone else.

➤ refer to Step Five in the two examples in Appendix B.

➤ start with the final Small Step and work backward. Ask yourself at each step "what do I need to do to make this happen?"

➤ remove yourself from the picture and ask, "If this was Joe what would he need to do?" Solving problems for other people is sometimes easier than solving your own problems.

Make the Small Steps as detailed as possible. Everything is easier to do when you have a step-by-step plan. With practice, you will move from baby steps to giant steps.

Small Steps are similar to a To Do list because many of the things you need to do can be done quite quickly and you can check them off when they are done. You don't have to get them all and get them right on the first go through. As you work through the steps, add steps if they make the priority more manageable.

Example: Small Steps

Money tends to be a Roadblock as well as a Resource. An Activity that involves getting or spending Money is a #1 Priority Activity for many people.

Key to a Balanced Life: Money

My #1 Priority Activity: Pay off my credit cards

Roadblocks: No Extra Money

Resources I have: Time
                      Determination

Role: Individual/Consumer

Small Steps would be:

Step One: Identify the credit card with the highest interest rate, not the highest balance.

Step Two: Call the bank that issued the card to find out if they have a credit card with fewer frills at a lower interest rate and transfer the balance to that card.

Step Three: Remove the card from my wallet, put it away some place safe, out of sight. A Safety Deposit box would be ideal. If you don't have a safety deposit box, place the card in a can of water and freeze it. A can cannot be microwaved. The ice will thaw slowly. You have time to decide if the pain of paying the bill is worth it before you add a new charge. Freezing your credit card is less drastic than cutting it up and throwing it away. Since it is less drastic, it is easier to do and you increase the probability you will do it.

Step Four: Pay the minimum balance due on all the rest of my cards (if applicable)

Step Five: Pay something extra on the frozen card. Charging something extra is how you got the bill in the first place; you are just working in reverse to pay it off.

Step Six: To pay $10.00 in one month of 30 days, all you have to find is 33 cents each day you don't spend on something else.

Accomplishing one priority builds Resources you can apply to the Roadblocks for your other priorities.

Small Steps Increase Your Resources

Resources you gain from paying off your credit card:

➢ The discipline you gain by not thawing the can.

➢ Peace of mind as the credit card balance declines.

➢ Pride in yourself as you get yourself out of the situation you are responsible for getting yourself into.

➢ Optimism when the credit card is paid off and the bill arrives in the mail with a zero balance.

➢ Freedom to accomplish one of your other keys that requires the Resource of Money.

Exercise: Small Steps

Write down all the actions you can think of for each of your #1 Priority Activities. Keep in mind those fifteen-minute blocks of time you initially set aside to work on your priorities.

Start anywhere in your list of Keys to a Balanced Life.

➢ Select one of your priorities with the Roadblocks, Resources, and Roles you have identified for it.

➢ Write down every action you can think of to accomplish this priority Activity with the Resources you have available.

➢ If you can't think of any small steps for this key, move on to the next priority. Ideas for one will inspire you for another.

➢ Review the actions you have written down. If you are unclear as to how you could accomplish them, find even smaller steps or actions that seem more manageable.

✓ REALITY CHECK

This exercise is the most difficult and time-consuming exercise in this book, but do not let the search for small steps bog you down. Keep going.

All of the small steps may not occur to you the first time you tackle a priority. Add them as you think of them. List what you can for each priority, and then move on to the next priority.

On the other hand, if you end up with too many options for a key, use your prioritizing technique of choice to find the Small Steps that fit with your Roadblocks, Resources and Roles. Everyone will have a unique set of steps.

Example:

Occupation: #1 Priority Activity:

I will have the ability to support myself in a stress free way.

Each of the small steps below would require many more small steps to make them manageable and achievable.

Potential Small Steps:

➢ Get a job
  ● Full time
  ● Part time
  ● Contract
  ● Temporary
➢ Create an occupation
  ● Freelance
  ● Paint, write, take photos
➢ Start a business

- Plant and sell flowers, vegetables
- Build furniture and sell it
➢ Buy a business
➢ Invest in the stock market.

Your choice would depend on your Occupational choice, Roadblocks, Resources, and Roles as well as how each choice would fit with your other nine Activities. The choice that is the least stressful for you is different from the choice that would be made by someone who defines and experiences stress in another way.

Small steps focus your "to do" activities toward a goal. Small steps don't all have to be done today, or this week. In the next section you will work on time horizons and time lines. This makes big projects, as well as small ones, manageable and within your reach.

STEP SIX:

A Commitment to Action

Priority Activities ➜ Roadblocks ➜ Resources

➜ Roles ➜ Small Steps ➜ **Action Plans**

➜ Motives ➜ Goals ➜ Mission

This step requires your commitment to when you are going to do the Small Steps you outlined in Step Five. Realistically estimate how much time you need to accomplish each step. Realistic thinking could be a Resource you have. Unrealistic thinking could be a Roadblock. This section covers

- Time Horizons and Time Lines
- Long-Term Planning
  - Birthdays as boundaries
- Short-term planning

When the Small Steps can be completed depends largely on the Resources you have right now and those you need time to acquire. If Procrastination is one of your Roadblocks, a very important Resource for you to apply is the Discipline to take action and keep moving.

Enlist the support of a friend to keep you on track if you don't think you have the discipline by yourself. If you do this, establish a schedule for reminders. It could simply be a weekly coffee session when you get together to discuss what is going on in your lives. When your coffee session has come and gone, you know another week has past. Your friend doesn't even have to say anything to you. The last thing you want to do is damage the friendship by putting the responsibility on your friend to "nag you".

Example: Estimating Time Lines

One of your small steps could require a five-minute action you can do today with immediate results, such as making a phone call to have a university course calendar mailed to you. One of the steps could need a year for its completion and another four years before you see results.

An example would be a decision to save for a year to go to university to start a four-year teaching degree.

Long-Term Planning

When you know who you are (Roles) and what you want to do (your ten Priority Activities), you are able to plan long-term. Your long-term time horizons serve as an outline for your small steps.

Example: Long-Term Planning

If you established your commitment to action on September 7, 2007, your long-term time horizon could be:

Within One Year	By September 7, 2008
Two to Five Years	September 7, 2008 to September 7, 2012
Six to Ten Years	September 7, 2012 to September 7, 2017
More than Ten Years	After September 7, 2017

✓ REALITY CHECK

The dates are measures of time passing.
The years have gone by, and will continue to go by.

Birthdays as Boundaries

Some of you will prefer to use your age to establish time horizons. This is another form of long-term planning because birthdays involve real dates.

Example: Attach Dates to Birthdays

By the time I'm 30	September 7, 2007
By the time I'm 35	September 7, 2012
By the time I'm 40	September 7, 2017
By the time I'm 55	September 7, 2032

If you are going to use your birthdays as boundaries, use actual dates. This defines your planning horizons. Your small steps make these long-term planning horizons manageable.

Short-Term Planning

Establish short-term time lines within your long-term time horizons.

Example:

If you established your commitment to action on September 7, 2007, your short-term time lines would be:

Within One Year:

Under Three Months by December 7, 2007

Three to Six Months by March 7, 2008

Six Months to a Year by September 7, 2008

Attach real dates in months and years to your planning horizons. Add weekly, daily and hourly small steps to make your timetable manageable. Use your 15 Minutes of Daily Action to get moving and keep moving as you identify the small steps you have decided to use to convert your Activities into goals.

✓ Reality Check

By establishing long-term plans,
you will avoid the temptation to become a quick-fix junkie.

Example: Attach completion dates to your small steps

To continue the example with the Key to a Balanced Life: Money, Role: Individual/ Consumer, attach completion dates to each of the Small Steps.

1) Five Minutes. Identify the credit card with the highest interest rate, not the highest balance by __Today__

2) Fifteen Minutes. Call the bank that issued the card and find out it they have a credit card with less frills at a lower interest rate by __Today__

3) Five Minutes. Remove the card from my wallet, put it away some place safe, out of sight. A Safety Deposit box would be ideal or freeze it by _Today__.

4) Five Minutes. Pay the minimum balance due on all the rest of the cards (if applicable)__one month from today__.

5) Five Minutes. Pay something extra on the card – even $10.00___one month from today__.

6) Forty-Five Minutes. Develop a cash flow by __enter a specific date__(one week from today). Know when, with the new payment schedule, your credit card will be paid off and you can congratulate yourself. You can then move on to the next key that requires Money as a Resource.

How much time do you need to complete the Small Steps for this #1 Priority Activity? Only One Hour and Twenty Minutes. (four five-minute, one fifteen-minute and one forty-five minute blocks of time).

How long will it take to accomplish this #1 Priority Activity? The answer depends on how much credit the bank has extended to you and how much you chose to use. By understanding where you are with your cash flow, you can look forward to the exact day you can celebrate. Just knowing there is an end in sight opens up your planning horizons for other priorities.

Exercise: Attach Completion Dates

➤ Estimate how much time you need for each Small Step.

➤ Use long-term and short-term planning techniques to attach completion dates to each of the Small Steps you wrote down for each of your ten priority Activities.

Your experience with action planning may have brought you this far before but your priority activities still didn't get accomplished. The next section presents more tools to help you gain the resources of persistence and determination.

STEP SEVEN:

Motives—the Act in Activities

Priority Activities ➜ Roadblocks ➜ Resources

➜ Roles ➜ Small Steps ➜ Action Plans

➜ **Motives** ➜ Goals ➜ Mission

In the process of goal setting, you are separate from the process. You are standing apart as you objectively view the changes you want to make in your life. You know where you've been and you know where you are. To help you find out where you are going, ask yourself "Why have I chosen these ten #1 Priority Activities?"

- Two Why's
- Putting the Act into Activities – a list of action verbs

Two Why's

For each of your ten #1 Priority Activities, you have said what you are going to do and when you are going to do it. Because these are just items on a list, even with the completion dates you added in Step Six, they don't have the power to motivate you towards their accomplishment.

This tool will help you uncover your motives. Ask yourself "Why is this a priority for me?" and "Why is it important enough that I feel it is a good use of my time?"

✔ REALITY CHECK

You need a motive. You need a " why?"

What are your expected outcomes? What has happened? What have you done? What have you gained? What is different? Why is it worth changing instead of just leaving things as they are? You are looking forward to results, either positive results or relief from negative results. Results are achieved through action. The following is a partial list of action verbs.

Action Verbs

Achieve	Encourage	Implement
Accomplish	Empower	Nurture
Acknowledge	Express	Network
Connect	Exercise	Promote
Communicate	Enjoy	Practice
Coach	Exchange	Provide
Create	Educate	Participate
Challenge	Focus	Reinforce
Develop	Facilitate	Research
Define	Guide	Support
Demonstrate	Inspire	Solve
Deliver	Increase	Translate
Dedicate	Improve	Teach
Design	Initiate	Understand
Establish	Investigate	Unite

Putting the Act into Activities

I will <u>do this.</u>

Why is this a priority for me?

Why is it important enough that I feel it is a good use of my time?

Because <u>I expect to get this positive result or avoid this negative result.</u>

Example One:

Key: Learning

Role: Student

#1 Priority Activity: Take a course in painting with water colors

I will take a course in painting with water colors.

Why is this a priority for me?

Why is it important enough that I feel it is a good use of my time?

Because by the end of the course, I will:

> ➢ Learn how to mix custom paint colors.
>> ● Gain a Resource: Skill
> ➢ Be familiar with the type of equipment needed to paint with watercolors.
>> ● Gain a Resource: Knowledge
> ➢ Connect with other people with similar interests.
>> ● Gain a Resource: Expand my network.

Example Two:

Key: Occupation

Role: Worker

#1 Priority Activity: Be a painter

I will occupy my time painting with water colors.

Why?

Because I will choose painting as my occupation to:

> ➢ Exercise my talents and express my creativity.
>> ● Gain Personal Growth, Satisfaction and Fulfillment
>> ● Avoid: Frustration
> ➢ Increase the flexibility of my working schedule
>> ● Gain: Freedom from schedules.

Exercise: *I Will, Why, Because*

In this exercise, use action verbs to describe the reasons, or the motives, that drive you.

Write your #1 Priority Activity in the form of an "I will" statement.

Ask "Why?"

Provide your motive with a "Because" statement using an action verb. The action verbs you can choose are limitless. Develop a why for each of your #1 Priority Activities.

STEP EIGHT:

Your Ten Goals for a Balanced Life

Priority Activities ➔ Roadblocks ➔ Resources

➔ Roles ➔ Small Steps ➔ Action Plans

➔ Motives ➔ **Goals** ➔ Mission

You are now ready to use your vision to see your future with your personal set of ten Goals for a Balanced Life. Because this set of goals is based on your #1 Priority Activities, you will be certain that there is a point to all the things you do that keep you busy. This step covers:

- Everyday Visions
- Converting Activities into Goals
- Developing the Picture
- Happy New Year! Time to Review your Progress
   - If you don't accomplish your goals

Everyday Visions

The following describes a vision you have possibly created in the past.

Example: An Everyday Vision

When you shop for and gather the ingredients for a dinner party, you have a vision of the dinner you will create. You plan and allow time to complete the small steps of slicing, dicing and cooking. You visualize the flowers, candles and the glasses sparkling on the table. You know what you will wear. There are many other items you consider including the time it will take, the equipment you will need to cook with, and the cleaning you have to do to prepare for the evening. These are Activities.

Goals have a big picture perspective and are reflected by your daily Activities. The need you are trying to satisfy by engaging in these Activities could be written as the following goal statement.

Example: Goal

Create a loving and supportive environment for my family and friends to fulfill my roles within my family and with my friends.

Converting Activities into Goals

You can use one, or a combination, of the tools outlined in the following five-part exercise to develop a clear picture of your big picture. Read through the exercises and examples and then choose the tools that work for you.

When you have completed this exercise, you will have one goal statement for each of your ten priorities.

Part One: Make Vision Statements

These six exercises and examples ask you to complete a statement visualizing yourself and your life a specific way, doing what you want, and enjoying what you do. The first example shows you how to change your #1 Priority Activities into goals.

Part Two: Draw a Picture

Use each of your ten #1 Priority Activities to assemble a drawing that depicts your ideal future life.

Part Three: Go on a Tear

This is a visual representation of your ten #1 Priority Activities. Couple it with a vision statement placed in a prominent place where you see it each day. It will be a powerful reminder of your goals.

If you are using a computer for the Activity of Goal Setting, you could also use your own photos and clipart to assemble your big picture. Save it as your desktop background.

Part Four: Do What You Love To Do

This is the simplest, yet the hardest thing to do. What you love to do impacts every one of your ten Keys to a Balanced Life.

Part Five: Aim! Focus! Snap the Picture!

This exercise brings all five of your senses into play. The example entitled "The Cabin in the Woods" describes the details of this moment in your future.

Exercise and Examples: Converting Activities into Goals

PART ONE: MAKE VISION STATEMENTS

1) Goal:

    My vision is to be known for _____.

    I want to be known for _____.

    Key to a Balanced Life: Occupation (how I occupy my time)

    Role: Community / Worker

    Priority Activity: My #1 Priority
    I will take one year away from the 9 to 5 routine of working for someone else to paint the pictures I always said I would paint.

    Why?

    Motive: I need to do this because:
    it is one of my "I have to try, before I die" commitments to myself.

    Goal: My vision for myself is to be known for *painting interpretational portraits that reflect the inner person rather than portraying just external appearances.*

2) Goal:

    My vision is to be recognized by _____ as the _____
    for the _____.

    Example:

    Goal: My vision is to be recognized by *the hospitality industry as the number one supplier of web-design services for the country.*

3) Goal:

    My vision is to create _____ for _____ around the world.

    Example:

    Goal: *My vision is to create a nurturing and supportive environment for my family wherever they are around the world.*

4) Goal:

I see myself as _____.

Example:

Goal: *I see myself as someone who can help others find answers by asking them questions.*

5) Goal:

My vision is to build _____ to _____ so _____ can share _____.

Example:

Goal: *My vision is to build strong relationships with my coworkers to encourage trust so we all can share the benefits of a family feeling in the workplace.*

6) Goal:

My vision is to _____ the desirability of _____ by choosing _____ as my occupation.

Example:

Goal: *My vision is to increase the desirability of the hospitality industry as a career option for people by choosing vocational consulting as my occupation.*

PART TWO: DRAW A PICTURE

You don't have to be an artist. Put yourself into the picture. Look at the picture from where you are outside of the big picture. What are you doing? Where do you fit? How do your ten keys show up in this picture?

PART THREE: GO ON A TEAR

Tear pictures from magazines and mount them on a large sheet of paper. Use magnets to arrange them on the fridge or frame them and hang them on the wall. You are looking for pictures that represent the ten keys. When you put them together, they form the big picture of your life as a whole.

Choose pictures of people doing things you want to do, places you want to go, and things you want to have. Find pictures of people together, and people alone. Include pictures that have moods to them as shown by scenes or colors. Glue photos of yourself into the pictures.

If your ten separate pictures don't form a big picture that makes you feel as if it is something you can do, you may be trying to create a fit among conflicting priorities. Re-examine the priorities you have chosen.

PART FOUR: DO WHAT YOU LOVE TO DO

Goal:

I love _____

Example:

Goal: *I love to be on stage entertaining people by singing.*

PART FIVE: AIM! FOCUS! SNAP THE PICTURE!

This is your chance to develop the snapshot vision of your future. If you need inspiration, refer to the Cabin in the Woods example that follows.

Use words to paint your picture. Describe:

➤ the vision with you in it.

➤ from left to right, or top to bottom or vice versa.

➤ the state of being that your surroundings represent, instead of your physical surroundings.

As well as sight, use your other four senses of taste, touch, smell and hearing to experience your vision.

I see myself doing this _____

I am visualizing / planning to do this _____

I am mentally feeling _____

I am emotionally feeling _____

I am physically feeling _____

I hear _____

I smell _____

I taste _____

I see _____

Incorporate a statement that reflects each of your #1 Priority Activities for the ten keys.

I can realize my goals for each of the ten Keys to a Balanced Life by doing these Activities:

1) Physical Health

2) Mental Health

3) Money

4) Fun

5) Family

6) Occupation

7) Good for My Soul

8) Giving Back to Society

9) Friends

10) Learning

Example: The snapshot vision of your future: The Cabin in the Woods

I want a nice little cabin on a lake where I can canoe becomes

➤ It is quiet, and peaceful here in the last days of summer now that the summer tenants have gone home. A crow cawing and the chattering of a squirrel are the only sounds that break the silence. I can hear the waves gently lapping the shore.

➤ The sun warms me as I sit outside on my porch in a big comfortable chair.

➤ I am wearing my favorite red sweater.

➤ The aroma of coffee combines with the smell of cinnamon from a freshly baked roll. This adds to my feeling of well-being.

➤ A warm wind is blowing off the lake. It carries the green smell of lakeshore grasses to the porch.

➤ I am feeling calm and relaxed. No one is placing demands on my time.

➤ I have simplified my needs and am living a comfortable life within my means. Having the summer bed and breakfast provides me with the opportunity to meet many new people from all over the world. As I get older, my circle of friends and acquaintances continues to expand. The money supplements my savings and pension.

> ➤ I am expecting my family to arrive this evening and I will walk to the market this morning to get some groceries for the weekend.

> ➤ This afternoon, I will cook and clean in anticipation of their arrival.

> ➤ I will cut some fresh flowers from my garden for the guestroom to make them feel welcome.

> ➤ I am looking forward to the silence of the first snowfalls when I will continue to work on my favorite project.

The more detail you can add to your vision and the more specific you can be, the easier it will be for you to re-create the vision in reality. How did you find this place, why did you decide to choose it? What kind of chair, what color and variety of flowers? Instead of my family list their names. What are you going to buy at the market? What are you going to cook? How will it smell and taste? What is your winter project? How is it going to benefit society? What will you learn? Details, details, details! Details make the picture clear and familiar and, therefore, easier to achieve.

Choose the tools that use your Resources to convert your #1 Priority Activities into Goal Statements.

Developing the Picture

Many of your unforgettable occasions, the best and the worst memories, are only snapshots of a moment or movies of a single occasion in your mind. When you get together with other people, it is nice to share these memories.

Many times, you view your future as a snapshot of the scene you visualize; however, unlike a snapshot, your life is dynamic. You are changing, even as you read this. Cells are growing and dying. Time is passing. You will never be any younger than you are right at this second. The scene will change as time passes and this will change your future. You spend the rest of your life in the future. The two-part goal setting process is your tool to shape your future.

Happy New Year! Time to Review your Progress

Throughout the year, you will add Activities to your one day list. As you add them, classify these new Activities under one of the Keys to a Balanced Life.

Some of your goals had one-year time lines and you have accomplished them. Now is the time to choose a new priority for that key from all the possible Activities that remain. Keep moving forward on the goals that included small steps with time lines longer than a year.

Select an annual date to sit down and review your progress on the goals you have established for each of the ten keys.

➤ Your annual vacation may be the only time you step back and re-evaluate your life. Continue to use the two-part goal setting process to keep balance in your life. Role: Individual, Keys to a Balanced Life: Physical and Mental Renewal, Priority Activity: Review my progress and work on my goals.

➤ You may want to select a weekend and go to a specific location away from the demands of day-to-day life. Role: Individual, Key to a Balanced Life: Mental Health, Priority Activity: Choose a set of goals / Review my progress.

➤ You may want to use your birthday as the date to congratulate yourself on your accomplishments. Role: Individual, Key to a Balanced Life: Spiritual Celebration, Priority Activity: Maintain an awareness of how far I have come before I focus on far I have to go.

➤ If you have a romantic partner, establish goals separately, and together. Use the anniversary of the day you met for your review. Role: Romantic Partner, Key to a Balanced Life: Family, Priority Activity: Annually review our progress, as individuals and as a couple.

At the end of one year, your Two to Five Year horizon is upon you. Based on your small steps, you have been working on this time horizon already.

Example: Review Dates

If you used September 7, 2007, as your start date, after one year has passed your review date is somewhere near September 7, 2008. Your planning horizons have changed to:

Two to Five Years	September 7, 2008 to September 7, 2012
Six to Ten Years	September 7, 2012 to September 7, 2017
More than Ten Years	After September 7, 2017

Establish short-term time lines within these longer time horizons. Keep the original dates.

Example:

Two to Five Years	September 7, 2008 to September 7, 2012
Under One Year	By September 7, 2009
Within Three Years	By September 7, 2011

Within Five Years from my start date   By September 7, 2012

If you like shorter time horizons, your time lines would be:

Under One Year   September 7, 2008 to September 7, 2009

Within three months   By December 7, 2008

Within six months   By March 7, 2009

Within nine months   By June 7, 2009

Within one year   By September 7, 2009

Your two to five year time horizon has four years, because one year has passed at the point of your one-year review.

✓ REALITY CHECK

The real dates in months and years you attached to your planning horizons remain unchanged.

If You Don't Accomplish Your Goals

Time passes. You work on your goals according to all the small steps you have put in place to achieve them. If you don't accomplish these small steps within the time frame you originally specified, do six things:

1) Move the step forward into the next time frame, rather than abandon it. Once three months have gone by, your time frame Three to Six Months has now become Under Three Months. Don't change the label, just move the item forward.

2) Review your Roadblocks and Resources. Do you need to add "too optimistic" as one of your Roadblocks and "be realistic" as one of your Resources? Apply Discipline and Persistence.

3) Examine the Small Steps you have established to achieve this Goal. Break them down further into smaller, more manageable steps.

4) Revisit the time estimates you have attached for doing and completing your Small Steps.

5) Re-evaluate the rest of the steps in the eight-step decision process for any opportunities that exist to complete this goal successfully.
Priority Activities ➔ Roadblocks ➔ Resources➔ Roles ➔ Small Steps ➔

Action Plans➜ Motives ➜ Goals ➜ Mission

6) Try again!

Example: Move the step forward into the next time frame

At your one-year review on September 7, 2008, if you didn't accomplish your goal, move your Small Steps forward into the next time frame.

> Goal: Within three years, lose 20% of my current body weight. I anticipate the positive benefit of enjoying a more active and healthy lifestyle.

> Small Step: Lose 10 pounds

> Within One Year   By September 7, 2008

If the date has passed when the Small Step was to be completed, change your time line to:

> Small Step: Lose 10 pounds

> Within One Year   By September 7, 2009

Review September 7, 2009.

You do, of course, have the option of abandoning this goal and going through all the steps to develop another Activity into another goal instead. As you learned earlier, different priorities produce different results. If abandoning goals becomes a pattern, you are using your time to start multiple options but are completing none.

The next section on Mission in Life statements is for those of you who have tried to write a personal mission statement in the past. It is also for those of you who are curious to find out what your mission in life is according to your goals.

Your Mission in Life.

Mission Control

Priority Activities ➔ Roadblocks ➔ Resources

➔ Roles ➔ Small Steps ➔ Action Plans

➔ Motives ➔ Goals ➔ **Mission**

Each of you has a unique mix of interests, skills and talents that attracts you to specific Activities. Your unwritten mission is guiding how you use these resources to engage in your everyday observable Activities. This section covers:

- What your mission reveals about your point of view

- Personal mission statements

- How to live everyday your way

- Your mission in life as your measure of how you are doing

- How to discover the unwritten mission statement that motivates you to choose your set of goals.

Your Point of View

As you are formulating your goals, it may occur to you that there is a point of view that is uniquely your own. Several people can choose exactly the same #1 Priority Activity to convert into a goal, but each person has their own vision of what it will be when it is completed.

Examples:

➤ Van Gogh, Rembrandt and Monet are all painters, but each had a unique vision of how to interpret the world. Their unique mission guided their vision—it was in control.

➤ Not all entrepreneurs start restaurants, not all athletes are football players, not all musicians are piano players and not all piano players play classical music.

✓ REALITY CHECK

Everyone has a unique mission, including you.

Personal Mission Statements

Writing a personal mission statement is a difficult and time-consuming task. Defining a mission that you feel embodies all you stand for is just about impossible.

Personal mission statements are intangible and have been instilled with the aura of having spirituality as their source. It is an awesome responsibility to feel that you could fail to fulfill your destiny if you don't successfully identify your mission in life.

Everyday Your Way

Don't spend one minute more than is absolutely necessary to identify your mission in life. To remove the air of mystery from your search, the Eight-Step Decision Process starts with the familiar—your everyday activities—and then builds up to the goals and mission that inspire your activities.

You can all remember the activities you did today and even the significant details of yesterday. By starting in the present, you can see the results you are getting now. You then pull the future into your planning horizons by understanding how your everyday activities fit into your bigger picture.

Instead of tackling the vague project of writing your mission in life, examine your day-to-day Activities. Study how you are spending the time of your life. What did your Activities tell you about what was important in your life when you converted them to goals? The example below describes how your goals could illustrate your Mission in Life.

The point from which you view your big picture is your mission. It is the reason you are here in the first place. It encompasses the things you hope people remember you for after your physical body is no longer here.

✓ REALITY CHECK

What you do each day is a reflection of your mission in life.

Example: **Your Mission**

My Unwritten Mission Statement

Key: Occupation

Goal: My vision is to be known for creativity and innovation in seeking solutions to business problems.

Mission in Life:
I will use the talents I have been Given.

Mission in Life:
I will always lend a hand where it is needed.

Mission in Life:
My success is derived from my ability to make others successful.

In the preceding example, one goal reflects three Mission in Life statements.

In the next example, three goals underlie one Mission in Life statement.

Key: Good for My Soul

Goal: I see myself as someone who can help others find answers by asking them questions.

Key: Giving Back to Society

Goal: My vision is to increase the desirability of the hospitality industry as a career option for people by volunteering as a resource to hospitality schools.

Key: Money

Goal: My vision is to work internationally with the hospitality industry as a knowledgeable source for identifying marketing solutions for their businesses.

Mission in Life:
I will light the candle of knowledge
and share my wisdom.

In this example, one goal inspires five Mission in Life statements.

Key: Mental Health

Goal: My vision is to build strong relationships with the people I work with to encourage trust. We can benefit from a family feeling when we are working together.

Mission in Life:
I will treat every person as part of my family of man.

Mission in Life:
I will prevent puppies from being kicked.
I will defend those who are unable to defend themselves.

Mission in Life:
I will live by the Golden Rule:
Do unto others as you would have them do unto you.

Mission in Life:
I will respect all living things.

Mission in Life:
I will value people before things.

In the next example, one goal underlies two Mission in Life statements.

Key: Family

Goal: My vision is to create a nurturing and supportive environment for my family wherever they are around the world.

Mission in Life:
I will do my utmost to raise children that are
contributing members of society.

Mission in Life:
I will ensure those I love know I love them
first, by my actions, and then my words.

In the following two examples, each Mission in Life statement arises from one goal.

Key: Learning

Goal: My vision is to be known for always approaching life with an attitude of curiosity.

Mission in Life:
I am committed to life-long learning.

Key: Physical Health

Goal: I love helping others to find new ways of dealing with the issues they face in life, particularly relating to their health, diet and exercise.

Mission in Life:
I will live fully and die contented.

Each goal can reflect more than one of your Mission in Life statements. Several of your Mission in Life statements can be a reflection of just one goal.

Interpret your goals as you feel they reflect what you believe in and how you live your life on a daily basis. What would your Mission in Life be for Fun and for Socializing?

Your Mission in Life serves as your internal measuring stick. Once you have chosen to live your life with ten Goals for a Balanced Life, you engage in Activities that are necessary to accomplish your goals. As you do so, you fulfill your mission in life.

✓ REALITY CHECK

By measuring the accomplishment of your goals against your mission in life, you receive reliable feedback on how you are doing.

At this point you have ten goals, one for each of the keys. They should be feeling like old friends now, because they are a reflection of who you are and what you want to do. These goals are based on your Activities, the things you do each day or things that you wanted to do someday that are important to you. What do they say that you value? What is your philosophy of life?

What do you believe in? Look back to the section in this book at how you measure yourself and your accomplishments.

Exercise: Your Mission in Life Statements

You have chosen your goals because you have a picture of how and what you want to be. Use these goals and refer to the example above to discover your unwritten mission statement. You should be pleasantly surprised at how easily your Mission in Life Statements occur to you now that you have chosen your ten Goals for a Balanced Life.

Your Mission in Life is your own unique point of view. It is the reason you have chosen the set of goals that you have chosen. No one but you can live your life in your way.

Last Thoughts on Goal Setting

With practice and experience, choosing daily Activities to support your Goals moves from a conscious and thoughtful state to the point where it is completely automatic. What once may have been baffling becomes routine. Choose daily Activities that provide balance in your life as they contribute to your Mission in Life.

When you think about it, you have had a lot of practice in setting and accomplishing goals. You searched for information to solve a problem and then you made decisions on how you were going to use that information to make the change.

Now, you know your daily activities are helping you to achieve your goals. Your goals are directly related to your Mission in Life. Choose your daily activities with all of your goals in mind as you strive for balance in your life.

Before you read this book, you might have found yourself at the end of the day saying, "I just don't know where the time went". Now, at the end of your life, whenever that may be, it is my sincere wish you will say, "I tried everything and did most of the things that were important to me".

APPENDIX A

Time Use – A Guideline

You may be in for some surprises as you keep track of how you spend your time in each of your roles. Whether you estimate how you spend your time, or you actually record how you spend your time for a two-week period, use fifteen-minute increments. If the time you spend is less than fifteen minutes, just use a stroke / and count five of them as fifteen minutes. This gives you an indication that you did spend at least some time in this area.

Why fifteen-minute increments? Fifteen minutes is one-quarter of an hour. Fifteen -minute increments help you develop an awareness of the importance of, and the limit to, the time available to you.

15 minutes a day, 7 days a week, 52 weeks a year is 5460 minutes or 91 hours per year, or one and three-quarter hours per week. How many times have you spent 15 minutes without knowing where it went?

At the end of two weeks, total the time you spent in each of your roles. If you used minutes, divide by 60 to arrive at the number of hours you used. Multiply by 26 to arrive at the total hours you need each year for each Role. (26 two-week periods in a year equals 52 weeks in a year. Plus one day).

Do you need more than the 8760 hours that are available to you in the year to meet your time commitments for your roles?

An example entitled The Time of Your Life illustrates a sample of roles, activities for those roles and the time the activities consume on an annual basis.

The Time of Your Life

Total Hours Available in a Year 8760					
Role	**Individual**				
Activity	**Hours**	**Hours Spent/Day**	**Total Hours Spent/Week**	**Total Hours Spent/Year**	**Balance Of Hours/ Year**
Sleep Daily	11pm–6am	7 Hours	5 Days /Week 35 hours/week	52 Weeks /Year 1820 hours/year	6940 Hours
Sleep Weekends	11pm–8am	9 Hours	2 Days/Week 18 hours/week	52 Weeks /Year 936 hours/year	6004 Hours
Total Time Spent Sleeping Include naps in your sleep time.				**2756 Hours**	Balance 6004
Breakfast 5 Days	6:00am–6:30am	One Half Hour .5	2.5 hours/week	130 hours/ year	
Breakfast Weekends	8:00am–8:30am	One Half Hour .5	1 hour/week	52 hours/ year	
Lunch 7 Days	12:00pm– 12:30pm	One Half Hour .5	3.5 hours/week	182 hours/ year	
Dinner 7 days	6:00pm–6:30pm	One Half Hour .5	3.5 hours/week	182 hours/ year	
Coffee X 2 x 7 days	.25 X 2	One Half Hour .5	3.5 hours/week	182 hours/ year	
Total Time Spent Eating (1)				728 hours/ year	Balance 5276
Personal Care	6:30am–7:15am	.75 hours/ day	5.25 hours/ week	273 hours/ year	Balance 5003
Physical Exercise	Daily 2 X 30 minutes	One hour/ day	7 hours/week	364 hours/ year	Balance 4639
Read	Daily 2 X 30 minutes	One hour/ day	7 hours/week	364 hours/ year	Balance 4275
Watch TV	Daily 2 X 1 hour	2 hours/day	14 hours/week	728 hours/ year	Balance 3547
Cook(10)	Daily Varies	2 hours/day	14 hours/week	728 hours/ year	Balance 2819
Dishes(10)	Daily Varies	One hour/ day	7 hours/week	364 hours/ year	Balance 2455

Lots of time, right?

Role	Individual				
Activity	**Hours**	**Hours Spent/Day**	**Total Hours Spent/Week**	**Total Hours Spent/Year**	**Balance Of Hours/ Year**
Beds Making	Daily	Varies .25 hours	1.75 hours/ week	91 hours/year	Balance 2364
Laundry	Weekly Varies		One hour/ week	52 hours/year	Balance 2312
Clean	Weekly		2 hours/week	104 hours/ year	Balance 2208
Garden (4)	Weekly 26 weeks	Varies	4 hours/week	104 hours/ year	Balance 2104
Fall Clean	Yearly	Varies	12 hours	12 hours/year	Balance 2092
Spring Clean	Yearly	Varies	12 hours	12 hours/year	Balance 2080
Role	**Individual Consumer**				
Car Care Wash, Gas	Weekly	Varies	One hour/ week	52 hours/year	Balance 2028
Car Care Maintain(3)	Quarterly	Varies	One hour /quarter	4 hours/year	Balance 2024
Hair Care	Bi-Monthly	Varies	2 hours	12 hours/year	Balance 2012
Groceries	Weekly	Varies	One hour/ week	52 hours/ year	Balance 1960
Spiritual Renewal	Weekly	Varies	One hour/ week	52 hours/ year	Balance 1908
Finances Eg Banking	Weekly	Varies	Half hour / week .5	26 hours/ year	Balance 1882
Renewal Eg Facial	Each Quarter	Varies	2 hours / quarter	8 hours/ year	Balance 1874
Spring/Fall Planting	Yearly	Spring/Fall	12 hours/ year	12 hours/ year	Balance 1862
House Painting	Yearly	Varies	24 hours/ year	24 hours/ year	Balance 1838
Vacation (5)	Yearly 2 weeks	24 hours/ day	168 hours/ week	336 hours/ year	Balance 1502

Role	Independent/Individual/Pet Owner				
Activity	Hours	Hours Spent/Day	Total Hours Spent/Week	Total Hours Spent/Year	Balance Of Hours/ Year
Feed / Litter	Daily AM	Half hour /day .5	3.5 hours/ week	182 hours/ year	Balance 1320
Groom	Monthly	Half hour / month .5	6 hours/ year	6 hours/ year	Balance 1314

Still lots of time?

Role	Worker	Based on 50 weeks			1314
Activity	Hours	Hours Spent/Day	Total Hours Spent/Week	Total Hours Spent/Year	Balance Of Hours/ Year
Regular Hours Daily	8am – 12 Noon and 1pm – 5pm	8 hours/day	40 hours/week	2000 hours/ year	(686)
Commute (2)	Daily X 2	1.5 hours/day	7.5 hours/ week	375 hours/ year	(1061)
Socialize At Work (8)	Daily	Half hour/day .5	2.5 hours/ week	125 hours/ year	(1186)
Overtime Hours	5pm-6pm Weekly	One hour/day	One hour/ week	50 hours/year	(1236)
Role	**Friend**				
Five Friends(9)	Monthly	3 hours /month X 5 friends	15 hours/ month	180 hours/ year	(1416)
Role	**Student/Learner Personal and Professional Development**				
Self-study	Daily	2 Half hours/ day	7 hours/week	364 hours/ year	(1780)
Seminars	Monthly	Varies	1 hour/month	12 hours/year	(1792)
Study Trips	Half Yearly		4 hours half yearly	8 hours/year	(1800)
Classes/ Lectures	Every 5 years				

Activity	Hours	Hours Spent/Day	Total Hours Spent/Week	Total Hours Spent/Year	Balance Of Hours/ Year
Role	Volunteer	No time allocated			
Role	Spiritual Being	See Spiritual Renewal under Individual above			
Miscellaneous Travel Time (based on 50 weeks) To pick up kids from school and drive them to their activities, gas stations, grocery stores, to visit friends and family, to pick up supplies for gardening and house maintenance					
Travel	Varies	Varies	7 hours/week	350 hours per year	(2150)

Roles	Family				(2150)
Activity	**Hours**	**Hours Spent/Day**	**Total Hours Spent/Week**	**Total Hours Spent/Year**	**Balance Of Hours/ Year**
Daughter/ Son	Weekly	Varies	2 hours/week	100 hours/ year	(2250)
D//S-in-law	Quarterly	Varies	2 hours/ quarter	8 hours/year	(2258)
Brother/ Sister	Half Yearly	Varies	8 hours/ half year	16 hours/ year	(2274)
B/S-in-law	Yearly	Varies	Included with Brother/ Sister – 8 hours		
Mother/ Father (6)	Monthly	Varies	4 hours/month	48 hours/ year	(2322)
M/F-in-law	Monthly	Varies	Included with Mother/ Father- 48 hours/year		
Wife/ Husband(7)	Daily	Varies .5	3.5 hours/week	182 hours/ year	(2504)
Grandparent	Monthly	Varies	Included with Mother/ Father-48 hours/year		

The section on the time shortfall offers a perspective on the 2504 hours you would be short if you lived the same life as the person in this example, even with the conservative estimates used above.

Notes to the above:

1) Eating does not include the time spent lingering at the table socializing with other persons present over a cup of coffee or glass of wine. This time is discretionary and is a choice on your part to spend it this way.

2) Many of you commute twice as long and this is reflected in your time log and totals. Based on 50 weeks times 5 days.

3) Car Maintenance assumes time to make the appointment and deliver the car to the station only, as you are not working on the car yourself.

4) Gardening assumes 26 weeks of spring, summer and fall garden maintenance.

5) Vacation time is recognized as being spent in other things you do but as it is discretionary time how it is spent is a choice on your part.

6) Mother/Father assumes grown children who do not accompany you on vacation. The picture would be quite different for those of you with children at home. This time should reflect one-on-one time with the children only, separate from Maintenance Activities.

7) Husband/Wife time is one-on-one time, not with one of you reading and one watching TV and not doing chores.

8) Work socializing is during non-work hours (lunch hour, after work).

9) Visiting friends is often combined with a meal.

10) Acknowledge that at work meals involve a tradeoff of money to purchase meals in exchange for this time.

APPENDIX B

The Eight Steps in Action: Three Examples

Example One: Blueprints for Accomplishing Goals

When you undertake and complete various projects, they are the result of careful planning and thoughtful decisions. As mentioned in Part I, these projects upset the balance in your life as you focus your time and attention on their accomplishment.

➢ Buying a car

➢ Planning a vacation

➢ Building a house

➢ Getting a university degree

All of these projects follow a blueprint as you move through the two processes of information search to solve your problem and decision-making.

Information Search to Solve your Problem

➢ You look at where you are today and decide if your current situation is working for you.

➢ You make a commitment to change some aspect of your life.

➢ You consider the roles you have and possibly enlist the help of an expert.

➢ You make the time to complete the necessary activities.

➢ You identify all your possible options.

Eight Steps to Choosing a Set of Goals

1) You narrow down your options by establishing priorities.

2) You consider everything that could stand in your way.

3) You apply the resources you have and identify those you need to obtain to overcome your roadblocks.

4) You assign roles to the ten Keys to a Balanced Life.

5) You identify all the small details required for the completion of your goals.

6) You establish a time frame for the completion of the project.

7) You focus on the solution you are seeking.

8) You have a vision or picture in your mind of the end result you desire.

Your Mission in Life

At first glance, the bigger picture represented by buying a car, building a house and many of your other projects isn't obvious. Actions that begin as noble objectives become lost in the hectic day-to-day business of life. A car is purchased to accommodate car seats for the safety of your child; a house is purchased to provide a stable home near good schools in a safe neighborhood.

These projects could show up as a mission in life statement such as:

*I see myself as the person
who is responsible for the safety and security of my family.
To that end, I will
provide them with the safest, most reliable transportation
and a home in the best neighborhood that my resources allow.*

The Eight Steps in Action

Example Two: Convert your #1 Priority Activity into a Goal

STEP ONE

Priority Activities ➔ Roadblocks ➔ Resources
➔ Roles ➔ Small Steps ➔ Action Plans
➔ Motives ➔ Goals ➔ Mission

From all the possible activities outlined in the Keys to a Balanced Life under Physical Health, identify the #1 Priority Activity you want to work on. (It is recommended you consult with your doctor prior to starting any new exercise program).

#1 Priority Activity: Walk One Mile Three Days Each Week

STEP TWO

Identify Your Roadblocks

> Priority Activities ➔ **Roadblocks** ➔ Resources
> ➔ Roles ➔ Small Steps ➔ Action Plans
> ➔ Motives ➔ Goals ➔ Mission

Roadblock One: I don't have jogging gear/sweat suit.

Roadblock Two: My summer runners are worn out, they hurt my feet when I walk.

Roadblock Three: Procrastination, this is new, I haven't done it before, I can't be bothered, it's raining (or too hot or…).

Roadblock Four: No instant results.

Roadblock Five: My schedule changed.

Roadblock Six: Is this worth it?

This is just an example. You all have Roadblocks that you can come up with as justifications or reasons why you cannot do something.

STEP THREE

Apply Your Resources

> Priority Activities ➔ Roadblocks ➔ **Resources**
> ➔ Roles ➔ Small Steps ➔ Action Plans
> ➔ Motives ➔ Goals ➔ Mission

Resource One: Equipment.
Loose, comfortable, layers. Experiment!

Resource Two: Knowledge of correct equipment.
Look up sporting goods stores or go to one you know about and let the experts look after you.

Resource Three: Values.
This is your #1 Priority Activity. You have told yourself it is important. You have committed to spend your time doing it. You anticipate a benefit – a positive outcome for yourself.

Resource Four: Self-discipline.

Results depend on the benefit you are seeking—increased stamina, increased energy, weight loss. Long periods of inactivity are only undone by long periods of exercise.

Resource Five: Time.

Re-schedule and apply self-discipline.

Resource Six: Self-esteem.

By the end of the first week, you will be walking one-half mile over three days. Three weeks from then, you will be walking one mile, three days per week.

STEP FOUR

In the Starring Role

> Priority Activities ➔ Roadblocks ➔ Resources
> ➔ **Roles** ➔ Small Steps ➔ Action Plans
> ➔ Motives ➔ Goals ➔ Mission
> Role: Individual
> Key: Physical Health

STEP FIVE

Take Small Steps

> Priority Activities ➔ Roadblocks ➔ Resources
> ➔ Roles ➔ **Small Steps** ➔ Action Plans
> ➔ Motives ➔ Goals ➔ Mission

Small Step One:

Decide which three days of the week you will walk. For this example, use Monday, Wednesday and Friday.

Small Step Two:

On Saturday morning, decide which clothes are going to be your walking outfit, loose comfortable layers. Light jacket, sweater or sweat shirt, t-shirts, slacks.

Small Step Three:

Get gas for the car. On Saturday, go to a sports store and get fitted with a pair of walking shoes and buy three pairs of sports socks. (Having the correct shoes makes all the difference in the pleasure of the walking experience, they serve as a reminder that they are a specialty piece of equipment (don't use them to cut the grass), and the financial outlay may serve to increase your commitment and involvement in the physical activity.

Small Step Four:
For the first week, walk one block and back (two blocks) on Monday, Wednesday and Friday (six blocks total or approximately one-half mile the first week). The commitment, not the distance, is important in forming a new habit.

Small Step Five:
For the second week, walk two blocks and back (four blocks) on Monday, Wednesday and Friday.

Small Step Six:
For the third week on Monday, Wednesday and Friday, walk four blocks and back (eight blocks) each day.

Small Step Seven:
On the fourth week on Monday, Wednesday and Friday, walk six blocks and back (12 city blocks are approximately one mile).

STEP SIX

A Commitment to Action

> Priority Activities ➜ Roadblocks ➜ Resources
> ➜ Roles ➜ Small Steps ➜ **Action Plans**
> ➜ Motives ➜ Goals ➜ Mission

Commitment One: Start my walking program.
                        Monday, April 15

Commitment Two: Walk one mile in one session.
                        Monday, May 06

Commitment Three: Have a new habit of walking one mile three times per week
                        Monday, May 13

STEP SEVEN

Motives—The Act in Activities

> Priority Activities ➜ Roadblocks ➜ Resources
> ➜ Roles ➜ Small Steps ➜ Action Plans
> ➜ **Motives** ➜ Goals ➜ Mission

Why is this a priority for me?
If I develop a lifestyle that includes exercise it will increase my physical well-being including maintenance of a weight that makes me feel good about myself, and it will increase my energy level and mental alertness.

Why is it important enough that I feel it is a good use of my time?
My physical capabilities underlie my ability to do everything else that is important to me.

STEP EIGHT

Your Ten Goals for a Balanced Life

> Priority Activities ➔ Roadblocks ➔ Resources
> ➔ Roles ➔ Small Steps ➔ Action Plans
> ➔ Motives ➔ **Goals** ➔ Mission

My Goal for the Key to a Balanced Life that is my Physical Health
I wish to realize the long-term benefits of staying active and healthy. Because I recognize I am not attracted to sports and do not consider Physical Ability, particularly coordination as one of my Resources, I will participate in activities to gain Physical benefits in a way I feel realistically fits with my skills, talents and capabilities.

Over the short-term, I know accomplishing this goal will make me feel better about myself in my Role as an Individual because I am taking time for myself. Taking time for myself to achieve a Physical Health Goal will instill Balance into this area of my life.

My Resources of Self-confidence and Self-esteem will be increased. I also know, from past experience, I will reduce my weight and have more energy. Increasing my Resources will help to overcome Roadblocks that I will encounter as I work on my other priorities.

Add a Mission in Life Statement for this goal, if you choose.

Just a note: If you get someone to join you on your walk, you could meet a Family or Socializing Goal. If you explore somewhere new while you walk, you could meet a Learning Goal. Each Goal can be intertwined with other goals to help you achieve balance in your life.

As a warning though, don't let "Other People's Participation" prevent you from undertaking your goals.

The Eight Steps in Action

Example Three: Break a Goal down into Activities

YOUR MISSION IN LIFE

Priority Activities ← Roadblocks ← Resources
  ← Roles ← Small Steps ← Action Plans
  ← Motives ← Goals ← **Mission**

I will bring joy to others by painting interpretational portraits that reflect the inner, as well as the outer person.
Key to a Balanced Life: Occupation
Role: Worker
What I want to do: Be a Painter

STEP EIGHT

Your Ten Goals for a Balanced Life

Priority Activities ← Roadblocks ← Resources
  ← Roles ← Small Steps ← Action Plans
  ← Motives ← **Goals** ← Mission

In order to feel fulfilled, I need to express my creativity. I have painted portraits before and it is what I love to do. I feel I am wasting the time in my life, and as I get older, I feel I am running out of time to do the things that are important to me. This makes me feel discontented and affects all of the other roles I have in my life.

My goal of becoming a painter will give me the freedom to do what I love, what is important to me, and I will feel fulfilled. As I strengthen my Resources of Confidence, Self-esteem, Courage and Risk-taking by using my talents and skills, I will be able to focus on the other keys and reinforce my other roles.

STEP SEVEN

Motives: The Act in Activities

Priority Activities ← Roadblocks ← Resources
  ← Roles ← Small Steps ← Action Plans
  ← **Motives** ← Goals ← Mission

By September 30 next year. Have my portraits well known. This will allow me to work from my home painting portraits.

I will make $$$ so I can earn my living by expressing my creativity and working to my own schedule.

STEP SIX

A Commitment to Action

Priority Activities ← Roadblocks ← Resources
← Roles ← Small Steps ← **Action Plans**
← Motives ← Goals ← Mission

Have three 24 inch x 30 inch canvases as demos finished by September 30, this year.

Have private commissions for three portraits by June 30, next year (promote as Other Occasions gifts).

By June 30, this year, know the owners of all the art galleries and art supply shops that could help me promote my work.

STEP FIVE

Take Small Steps

Priority Activities ← Roadblocks ← Resources
← Roles ← **Small Steps** ← Action Plans
← Motives ← Goals ← Mission

1) On February 15, find out who the popular portrait painters are in my city and how much they charge.
   Roadblock: Who has the information I need?
   Resource: Time, Knowledge

2) Make a list of possible subjects for my canvases by February 21, this year.
   Roadblock: Procrastination
   Resource: Self-discipline

3) Decide which subject to choose by February 24, this year.
   Roadblock: Too many things to do
   Resource: Discipline, Establish Priorities

4) By February 28, this year. Call to find out where the art supply shops are in my area. Meet the owners. Tell them what I can do.

Roadblock: When are they in?
Resource: Time, Self-discipline, and Talent

5) Buy the canvas, the paints, brushes and other supplies to do this first painting of this year by February 28, this year.
Roadblock: None
Resource: Time, Money

6) Start the painting on March 2, this year. Spend four hours, 9:00am to 1:00pm working on it.
Roadblock: None
Resource: Equipment, Skill, Talent, Time

7) On March 2, this year, estimate how much time will be required to complete this canvas and schedule appointments with myself to get it done by my estimated deadline of April 30, this year.
Roadblock: Procrastination
Resource: Self-discipline

8) On March 15, this year. Go to the nearest gallery and meet the owner and continue to meet one gallery owner per week to promote my work and myself.
Roadblock: Lack of confidence
Resource: Self-confidence, Self-esteem, Courage

9) On April 14, this year. Decide on the subject for my second canvas.
Roadblock: Too many things to do
Resource: Priorities

10) Buy the needed paints for the second canvas by April 30, this year.
Roadblock: None
Resource: Time, Money

11) April 30, this year. Finish first canvas, start second demo canvas, and start third two months after. Have all three demo canvases done by September 30, this year.

STEP FOUR

In the Starring Role

Priority Activities ← Roadblocks ← Resources
  ← **Roles** ← Small Steps ← Action Plans
  ← Motives ← Goals ← Mission

Role One: Worker   Key to a Balanced Life: Occupation

| Role Two: | Individual | Key to a Balanced Life: Good for My Soul |
| Role Three: | Student | Key to a Balanced Life: Learner |

STEP THREE

Apply Your Resources

Priority Activities ← Roadblocks ← **Resources**
  ← Roles ← Small Steps ← Action Plans
    ← Motives ← Goals ← Mission

Resource One: Time
I will commit to one year away from the 9 to 5 routine.

Resource Two: Money
I have enough money monthly and can work in the evenings when there is no natural light for painting if I need more money.

Resource Three: Equipment
I have an easel, brushes, paints and other supplies.

Resource Four: Skills
I have learned painting techniques.

Resource Five: Talent
The portraits I have painted over the years have been admired.

Resource Six: Knowledge
I can talk to people and they can sell for me.

Resource Seven: Self-discipline
I know I am able to keep myself motivated.

STEP TWO

Identify Your Roadblocks

Priority Activities ← **Roadblocks** ← Resources
  ← Roles ← Small Steps ← Action Plans
    ← Motives ← Goals ← Mission

Roadblock One:	I have to work
Roadblock Two:	I need to pay my bills
Roadblock Three:	I would need equipment
Roadblock Four:	I've never done this before

Roadblock Five:	I'm not good enough
Roadblock Six:	I don't know how to sell
Roadblock Seven:	Who am I fooling, I can't do this now.

STEP ONE

All About Priorities

Priority Activities ← Roadblocks ← Resources
  ← Roles ← Small Steps ← Action Plans
  ← Motives ← Goals ← Mission

Choose Be a Painter as my #1 Priority Activity from all the possible Occupations I have listed from my brainstorming session.

Ask: Why Does This Appeal to Me?
   I want to work for myself
   It would let me express my creativity
   I could work from home
   I could establish my own daily schedule
   I would look forward to working each day.

APPENDIX C

Time Use Grid Samples

INTERACTIVE ROLES

Primary Roles

Roles of No Choice

Primary Family Role _____

Relationship with _____

Activities include face-to-face, telephone and written communications

Activity	Hours	Hours Spent/Day	Total Hours Spent/Week	Total Hours Spent/Year	8760 Hours/Year
Balance of Hours:					

INTERACTIVE ROLES

Domino Roles

Roles of No Choice

Domino Family Role _____

Relationship with _____

Activities include face-to-face, telephone and written communications

Activity	Hours	Hours Spent/Day	Total Hours Spent/Week	Total Hours Spent/Year	8760 Hours/ Year
Balance of Hours:					

INTERACTIVE ROLES

Secondary Roles

Roles of Choice

Secondary Family Role _____

Relationship with _____

Activities include face-to-face, telephone and written communications

Activity	Hours	Hours Spent/Day	Total Hours Spent/Week	Total Hours Spent/Year	8760 Hours/Year
Balance of Hours:					

INTERACTIVE ROLES

Community Roles

Roles of Choice

Community Role _____

Relationship with _____

Activities include face-to-face, telephone and written communications

Activity	Hours	Hours Spent/Day	Total Hours Spent/Week	Total Hours Spent/Year	8760 Hours/Year
Balance of Hours:					

INTERACTIVE ROLES

Community Roles

Roles of Choice

Worker
Include: regular hours (excluding meals), overtime hours including work extracurricular Activities-mandatory (excluding meals), Socializing with co-workers including extracurricular Activities (formal and informal—ball games or drinks etc), and your commute to work and commute from work.

Student/Learner
Include: scheduled class time, homework, self-study, reading non-fiction related to your area of specialty, lectures, seminars, workshops-related or unrelated to your specialty, on-line workshops, field trips, practicing.

Friends
Include Activities with Friend One, Friend Two, etc.

Group, Organization, Club Member or Volunteer
Include teams, organized religion.

INDEPENDENT ROLES

Individual Roles

Individual Role _____

Activity	Hours	Hours Spent/Day	Total Hours Spent/Week	Total Hours Spent/Year	8760 Hours/Year
Balance of Hours:					

Include rest, sleep, eat regular meals and snacks, daily personal maintenance, daily household maintenance, seasonal household maintenance, maintenance of your finances, yard and garden maintenance, spiritual celebration, taking a mental holiday and consumer–include maintaining your health and doctors appointments, maintenance of your pet, the time you spend on your entertainment and your regular and seasonal vehicle maintenance.

Index

Reader Feedback

Key: Giving Back to Society

Role: Individual: Writer

Goal: My vision is to be known for writing books that share what I have learned, so people don't have to spend the time of their lives re-inventing the wheel.

We would appreciate your comments regarding *A Clear and Certain Future, An Integrated Life Planning Process* and any suggestions you have to improve it.

Please indicate whether your comments can be used in future editions.

Email: glennascheesman@netzero.net

ISBN 142510681-1